AEI LEGISLATIVE ANALYSES

*Balanced analyses of current proposals before the Congress, prepared with the help of specialists in law, economics, and government*

# Telecommunications Law Reform



1980
96th Congress
2nd Session



AMERICAN ENTERPRISE INSTITUTE
*for Public Policy Research*
*Washington, D.C.*

ISBN 0-8447-0227-7
Legislative Analysis No. 12, 96th Congress
February 1980

BAF 7-11-80

# Contents

# 1

## Introduction

According to some experts, more than half of the wages paid in the United States and nearly half of the nation's $1.8 trillion gross national product stem from the production, processing, and distribution of information goods and services.[1] The telephone plays a pivotal role in our "information society," a society whose wealth depends on the rapid flow of information throughout the economy. Almost all—94.5 percent—of our households are served by the telephone through 170 million telephone instruments and 22,000 switching centers connected by more than a billion circuit miles of wire and radio paths extending to every city and hamlet in the nation. This telephone system handles more than 600 million calls every day.[2]

The telephone system we take for granted grew, for the most part, as a protected, regulated monopoly. Each operating company was given exclusive authority to provide telephone service in a particular geographic area. One company, American Telephone and Telegraph Company (AT&T), together with its affiliated operating companies, accounts for a very high percentage of the telephones in offices and homes.

However, recent rapid technological innovations and the current movement toward "deregulation" have increased the pressure to allow more competition in communications services for homes and offices than in the past. Pending legislative proposals to accomplish this could have a profound effect on the nation's system of communications. Provisions of bills for the deregulation of radio communications have met substantial opposition and appear less likely to win acceptance at this time. For that reason, this analysis will not deal with proposals related to regulation of broadcasters but will examine arguments for and against the major changes proposed for the nonbroadcast part of the nation's domestic telecommunications market.

Deregulation of the domestic telecommunications industry is similar in principle to deregulation of the airlines. Those who propose deregulation would permit new competitors to enter the market; competitive forces would set prices and levels of service, subject to protective regulatory measures while the market shifts to full competition.

However, the analogy to deregulation of airlines is imperfect. The telecommunications industry is more capital intensive than is the airlines industry. Innovation in telecommunications cuts costs faster and increases demand more rapidly than does innovation in the airlines industry. Existing plant and equipment become obsolete more rapidly in telecommunications than in the airlines industry and render the technological assumptions on which regulation is based more quickly obsolete.

When deregulation of the airlines industry was being discussed, some analysts feared that it might lead to a series of mergers and a surviving dominant airline. In the nonbroadcast segment of the domestic telecommunications industry, one telephone system already has approximately 85 percent of the business. Thus, anyone who expects that competition will spring up to substitute for regulation must make a greater leap of faith when dealing with the telecommunications industry than when discussing airlines and most other industries.

Deregulation of both the telecommunications and the airlines industries has one characteristic in common. If Congress eliminates the relevant government regulatory commission, it eliminates a scapegoat. Then if anything goes wrong citizens will complain to members of Congress, who will be less able to blame conditions on a government agency. Telecommunications services are used by almost everyone in the United States and a reduction in availability or in quality of service would be more likely to trigger complaints from many people than is true in the airlines industry.

# 2

## Background

### Industry Structure

The domestic common carrier telecommunications industry is dominated by the telephone sector. The Bell Telephone System, the nation's largest supplier of telephone service, had 1977 operating revenues of $37 billion; its plant had a gross value of almost $104 billion. By contrast, the telegraph portion of the telecommunications industry is much smaller: Western Union Telegraph Company, which until recently was the monopoly provider of telegraph services, had operating revenues in 1977 of $555 million and gross plant valued at nearly $1.8 billion. Other domestic telecommunications sectors, such as specialized common carriers, value added carriers, and domestic satellite carriers, are each even smaller than this.[3]

The Bell Telephone System accounts for 82 percent of the domestic telephone service, measured by the number of telephone instruments, and 84 percent of the domestic telephone operating revenues. The Bell System dwarfs even the largest industrial corporations. For example, it employs more people (over 900,000), has more shareholders (approximately 3 million), and owns more vehicles (170,000) than any other company. Twenty-five Bell operating telephone companies (the Bell parent company, American Telephone and Telegraph Company, owns a majority of stock in 23) and about 1,600 small independent telephone companies provide local exchange service throughout the United States on a monopoly basis. The so-called independent telephone companies, many of which are owned by cooperatives or municipalities, serve about half of the U.S. land area in providing about 18 percent of the domestic telephone service as measured by the number of telephone instruments.

In addition to the parent corporation (AT&T) and the operating telephone companies, the Bell System includes the Long Lines Department, which provides long distance telephone and other intercity services; Western Electric Company, an unregulated manufacturing and supply concern wholly owned by AT&T; and Bell Telephone Laboratories, an unregulated company owned jointly by AT&T and Western Electric.[4]

### Regulatory Authority

The regulation of interstate telephone, telegraph, and cable communication activities was first entrusted to the Interstate Commerce Commission by the

Mann-Elkins Act of June 18, 1910. In 1934 regulation of interstate and foreign communication by wire and radio was lodged with the Federal Communications Commission (FCC).[5]

Section 1 of the Communications Act of 1934 stated that Congress intended "to make available, so far as possible, to all the people of the United States a rapid, efficient, nation-wide, and world-wide wire and radio communications service with adequate facilities at reasonable charges." Section 201 required that common carriers furnish interstate and foreign communications services upon reasonable request and establish physical connections for communications on through routes with other carriers, if the FCC determined this to be in the public interest. Section 214 regulated entry of carriers into the market. A carrier could not construct, extend, or use a line subject to FCC jurisdiction until the FCC issued a certificate finding that the present or future public convenience and necessity required or would require construction and operation of the lines. The FCC was given authority to require communications common carriers to build adequate facilities for the expeditious and efficient performance of their services as common carriers. The FCC was to regulate rates—regulation that would prevent a carrier from exploiting its monopoly position. Regulation of intrastate communications activities remained with the states though the area subject to FCC authority to the exclusion of state regulation has been expanded by court decisions. The states have generally engaged in a pattern of regulation of intrastate communications services much like that outlined in the federal law.

## Pricing Policies

Communications carriers subject to rate regulation are entitled to earn a fair rate of return on the net value of the property they use to serve the public. In general terms this requires a rate of return which will compensate the carrier and investors for the risks involved in providing services. The carrier is entitled to earn enough to maintain its credit standing, attract additional capital as appropriate, and provide earnings comparable to businesses with corresponding risks.[6]

Communications carriers subject to state regulation generally have computed overall revenue requirements statewide in setting rates. However, the pricing to the public of particular services has generally been set on a basis other than the arithmetically delineated unit cost, partly because of the difficulty of allocating "fixed" or "common" costs precisely. Business telephone rates, for example, historically have been set most often on a "value of service" basis. Rates for business telephones are higher than residential rates, for example, not only because business users make greater demands on the telephone system but because arguably the value of the service to them is greater.[7] Thus, the price of one class of telephone service may be less than its cost to the telephone company; in effect, its users enjoy a subsidy from other services. (Of course the extent to which business subscribers will continue to pay higher rates than others depends in part on the availability, cost, and convenience of substitute services.) Some users get an even greater subsidy because long distance calls within a single state are commonly priced according to a uniform schedule which reflects cost averaging, though the degree of averaging varies from place to place.[8] Thus, the rates for calls of the same distance between different points are frequently the same even though the costs of providing the services may vary greatly. Cost averaging may be explained in part by the greater cost of billing by distance. Unit costs are lower on a much used route so callers using such routes may subsidize callers on a less used route. Local rates are frequently averaged among each company's exchanges within a state, usually with some allowance for added costs for rural lines and added value of services for users with access to large populations within an exchange or metropolitan area. Rates for all interstate long distance calls of the same class and distance are also averaged; the total costs allocated to interstate service is recovered through a single rate structure applied to all sections of the country.[9]

Additional opportunity for cross subsidy exists in the allocation of costs as between intrastate and interstate facilities. A typical interstate long distance call involves costs for the subscriber's local exchange in placing the call to the interexchange point with Bell's Long Lines Department; the costs of the interstate facilities of the Long Lines Department; the costs of the receiving interexchange point; and the costs of the local exchange which receives the call and routes it to the person called. For the purpose of allocating costs, each phone company assumes that it receives as many interstate calls as it places. Therefore, the division of costs is between the exchange that originated a call and Bell System Long Lines. Sums collected by the companies originating interstate calls form a pool of revenues, the division of which is administered under jurisdictional separations procedures by Bell Long Lines. Allocation of the pool of revenues derived from interstate business necessarily involves a determination of how much of an operating company's local investment was really utilized in essentially interstate rather than local activities. Allocations from the pool of revenues to the 1,600 independent telephone companies, referred to as settlements, are based either on individual studies of the volume, distance, and duration of interstate calls or on a schedule of averages. Because billions of dollars of costs common to many services rendered by the communications carriers must be assigned to services to which they are not directly attributable, those who design and approve the separations formulas have substantial latitude to allocate costs and hence separation payments in a variety of ways.[10] The sums paid to the 1,600 independent operating companies under the separations procedure, according to one FCC commissioner, account for between 35 and 70 percent of the total revenues of these companies.[11]

After payments have been made to the independents, the Bell companies divide the money remaining in the pool of revenues. Payments to Bell operating companies originating long distance calls cover reimbursement for their expenses in providing interstate services and an allocation for profit. The amount of profit corresponds to the interstate investment reported by that company as compared with the total interstate investment of all Bell operating companies.

Local service is the biggest part of the telephone business. One witness told a congressional committee that the investment of operating companies in this area amounts to $90 billion out of a total investment in the U.S. telephone industry of $120 billion.[12] FCC's Common Carrier Bureau estimates that separations payments amounted to $3.5 billion in 1978.

According to one estimate, local residential telephones are used less than twenty minutes a day on the average, and there are fewer opportunities to lower costs through sharing of equipment and through economies of scale for local service than is true with long distance traffic. Thus, the most dramatic changes in telephone costs have been in the long distance market.[13] Telephone company officials contend that because of rate averaging, value-of-service pricing, and agreed-upon separations, substantial cross subsidies favor residential users and users in low-density areas. Rural telephone cooperatives may get as much as half of their revenues from the Bell System.[14]

John de Butts, chairman of AT&T, testified in 1977 that interstate long distance activities contributed $3 billion a year to the common cost of local telephone service, or 55 cents of each interstate long distance call charge.[15] Alfred E. Kahn, then chairman of the New York Public Service Commission, testified that he had no reason to question the amount of the cross subsidy, and also said that intrastate long distance calls also subsidized local residential services.[16] On the other hand, Richard E. Wiley, chairman of the FCC, testified in 1977 that it was not clear that business users were subsidizing residential telephone users.[17]

The telephone companies and state regulatory authorities defend subsidies to residential users on the ground that they help meet the Communications Act's mandate of providing universal service at reasonable charges. Others contend the Bell System takes earnings from its monopoly services to subsidize its services that are in competition with newcomers to the communications field.[18]

### Competitive Pricing

With the advent of competition in the communications marketplace, the prices charged for competitive services by the Bell System as the major supplier of such services have become a primary concern of companies that seek to compete with Bell. The pricing of communications services and equipment by those competing with Bell is obviously of concern to the Bell System. This section will cite only a few of the recent cases involving the pricing of competitive services to illustrate some of the problems involved and the regulatory response.

The applicable statute prohibits unjust and unreasonable discrimination in charges and practices for like services. Communications carriers may not give any unreasonable advantage to certain customers or subject anyone to an unreasonable disadvantage in charges or practices.[19]

The Bell System fears that its competitors will concentrate on serving high-density routes that offer the most potential for cost savings and that Bell will be unable to compete successfully with lower rates unless it abandons its past practice of maintaining uniform nationwide pricing for its services. Bell is still burdened with expensive facilities to serve sparsely populated areas of the country. Thus it feels that it should be allowed to employ pricing methodology for competitive services that will let it meet the competition of carriers that employ much smaller investments to serve only selected routes. Bell's competitors fear Bell's advantages of tremendous size and market penetration. They want to make sure that Bell's prices are not so low as to make entry into the communications market unprofitable or to drive out existing competitors. Bell can offer unusually low prices, according to competitors, if it is able to use profits from its monopoly services to subsidize its competitive services.

When private microwave systems began to be a competitive threat, AT&T responded in 1955 by issuing its first bulk-rate private line tariff. This tariff offered discounts of up to 28 percent, by one estimate, for customers who rented a substantial number of private lines from AT&T as compared with the rate to customers who rented a single line. The FCC investigated these bulk rates and concluded in 1961 that the rates discriminated against the small-volume user, because there was no demonstrated difference between the cost of furnishing a number of lines to one customer and the cost of providing the same number of lines between the same points for different customers.

In late 1960, after the FCC had authorized the development of private microwave communications systems in the *Above 890* proceeding, AT&T offered a new bulk message telecommunications service (MTS) rate structure for Wide Area Telephone Service (WATS). This rate structure allowed a customer to make an unlimited number of calls within a defined geographic area at a flat monthly rate. In January 1961, AT&T filed a four-tier multiple channel private line bulk-rate tariff called Telpak. The customer could lease 12, 24, 60, or 240 channels (Telpak A, B, C, or D) at varying discounts of up to 85 percent off the cost of individual private line rates. A competitor and a communications equipment manufacturer protested that Telpak was not a new service but was simply a bulk pricing discount that could not be justified under the statute by the costs involved. AT&T argued that costs for a bulk offering would be less than for individual private lines because use would be concentrated in high-density routes and because most customers would not use all of the bulk capacity they had ordered. It contended that the rates were a reasonable response to the threat of cream skimming by competitors and to pressures from large-volume users for the establishment of a private line offering.

In 1964 the FCC ruled that the rates for Telpak A and B were not justified by competitive necessity and were unlawful. It required AT&T to submit additional evidence to prove that the rates for Telpak C and D would produce enough revenues to cover costs. In 1965 the FCC ordered AT&T to include Telpak C and D offerings in a cost study ordered in another proceeding, to determine whether low rates for competitive services were being subsidized by higher rates charged for monopoly services such as MTS. The results of this "Seven-Way Cost Study" showed that Telpak was earning a 0.3 percent rate of return as compared with 10.1 percent for WATS services. The FCC ruled in 1976 that rates for Telpak C and D were noncompensatory and were not justified by competitive necessity.

The *Telpak* decision also dealt with how to determine whether a rate charged for communications services is compensatory. AT&T argued that it should be allowed to meet competition by calculating rates based on a long-run incremental cost (LRIC) methodology employed for that service alone, rather than on the basis of the fully distributed cost (FDC) method that requires rates for competitive services to reflect historical costs such as existing plant and equipment. (For additional discussion of LRIC see the section "Fairness in Competition" below.) AT&T contended that if the FCC insisted on using the FDC methodology, this would create a protective umbrella over the rates of its competitors and limit AT&T's ability to compete.

The FCC criticized the LRIC methodology advocated by AT&T because it was based on a mere forecast of the marginal cost of providing the new service and was likely to involve recovery of costs over a longer period of time than FCC thought proper. The FCC also objected to using different cost methodologies for different services. Assigning historical costs to monopoly services such as MTS would let Bell price monopoly services at whatever level was necessary to satisfy Bell's total revenue needs. Competitors regarded LRIC pricing as a form of predatory price cutting designed to drive them from the market. Bell considered it an appropriate response to competitors who would serve only the most heavily used routes, thus, in Bell's view, engaging in cream skimming. The FCC rejected use of the LRIC methodology and concluded that the FDC methodology was the most consistent with the statutory mandate to ensure just, reasonable, and nondiscriminatory rates.

In 1969 the Bell System made an experimental bulk-rate offering designated as Series 11,000 Service, with some advantages over the Telpak rates. The service was offered in forty-seven major cities in seven northeastern states. Competitors claimed that Bell lost money on this offering. AT&T argued that this offering responded to the FCC's decision on Telpak by permitting smaller users to share channels and that the Series 11,000 tariff was not designed to injure competitors. AT&T provided cost data to show that the new rate would yield revenues 20 percent above the costs of discrete facilities required to provide the service. Although the FCC permitted the tariff to take effect, AT&T did not offer the service after 1972.

In 1973 AT&T offered a Hi-Lo tariff that for the first time did not use rate averaging. The tariff offered lower rates for traffic in high-density centers and over high-density routes. This tariff was another response to competition from specialized carriers. Critics claimed that cost data and market projections submitted by AT&T were inadequate to justify the rates and that the carrier refused to disaggregate its supporting data so the FCC could determine whether each of the three rates involved was lawful. AT&T claimed that its Hi-Lo tariff was a valid competitive response, that the supporting data were as refined as possible, and that these data showed the rates were compensatory. In January 1976, the FCC held that the cost projections submitted were not sufficient to justify the differences in rates and instructed AT&T to submit a new set of rates.

In 1972 AT&T sought authority to build and operate a five-city system for private line data transmission, called Dataphone Digital Service (DDS), to compete with an all-digital network proposed by Datran. The FCC permitted construction and in 1974 authorized AT&T to operate the network on the condition that it justify the rates to be charged. In 1977 the FCC concluded that the earnings from this service were far below the cost of capital and thus were noncompensatory. Critics claimed that AT&T overstated the volume of business available in trying to justify its rates. They also charged that AT&T overestimated the competitive threat and thus set rates that were anticompetitive and so low as to require subsidy from other Bell service offerings and to force Datran into bankruptcy. AT&T responded that its rates were based on exhaustive studies and were calculated to be compensatory. The FCC delayed implementation of the service.[20]

These examples illustrate some of the problems in setting and regulating rates for competitive communications services. Clearly a significant problem is involved in assuring fairness to the major supplier of communications services and to its competitors as well, when the major supplier provides both monopoly and competitive services. The FCC has recently proposed the elimination of rate filings for all but dominant carriers. This approach, which is also proposed by some bills now pending in Congress, would speed up the offering of new services by competing carriers. Whether Western Union would be classed as a dominant carrier having a market position that might enable it to earn excessive amounts will not be known until the conclusion of this FCC proceeding.

## Effect of Advances in Technology

For many years after the invention of the telephone, communications technology was relatively stable and communications companies operating as regulated monopolies generally offered a single method of communication, such as telephone or telegraph. In recent years, however, developments in technology have wrought changes which have important implications for the future of telecommunications. Wiley has identified four developments of particular importance to telecommunications.[21] (1) Microwave radio transmission made possible high-capacity, low-cost, nationwide interconnection of local telephone exchange systems as well as special-purpose intercity networks. (2) Digital computer electronics technology (using high-speed on-off electrical signals rather than constantly varying continuous analog signals as commonly used for voice transmission by telephone) has brought a major market for data communications to the forefront and in addition has helped make handling of basic telephone communications more efficient. (3) Solid state electronics has helped reduce the cost, size, and power consumption of electronic equipment; these reductions have made it possible to do many things that were not previously practical. (4) Communications satellites relay large numbers of messages among widely separated locations on the earth's surface at lower cost and with greater reliability than had been possible with high-frequency ground-based radio transmission or submarine cables. Long distance voice communication by satellite provides a new dimension in telecommunications, it is said, in that cost is independent of distance.[22]

Traditional distinctions between written and voice telecommunications, between voice and video, between private line services and public message services, between data and voice transmission, and between computer technology and service on the one hand and communications services on the other are being broken down.[23] The elimination of these distinctions and the progressive reduction of certain costs as a result of technological advances, according to proponents of telecommunications law reform, make competition with the established telephone companies feasible.[24] The technology now exists for electronic delivery of first class mail, electronic transfers of funds, digital-data and other message services, and pay television. Technological innovation, many claim, has made the regulatory framework established by the Communications Act of 1934 obsolete.

## Decisions Affecting Competition

In evaluating legislative proposals that would effect basic changes in the regulation of telecommunications common carriers and mandate greater competition it is helpful to survey the decisions of the FCC and the courts which have altered the previous norm of essentially monopoly provision of telecommunications and related services. The FCC has consciously promoted competition over the last several years. Until recently the principal emphasis has been on competition in two areas—the provision of terminal equipment and the provision of interstate private line services.

**Terminal Equipment.** The telephone companies had long furnished the instruments used by customers as a part of their regulated monopoly service, and their tariffs typically prohibited connection of any device not supplied by the company.[25] The telephone companies feared that connection of "alien" equipment might damage the sensitive and complex system and degrade the quality of service for many subscribers. The FCC accepted this reasoning when it declined to sanction the use of the Hush-A-Phone, a plastic cup-like device placed on the telephone handset to funnel the speaker's voice into the instrument, to facilitate privacy of conversation, and to screen out noise. On review, however, the U.S. Court of Appeals concluded in 1956 that the telephone company tariffs were an unlawful interference with the subscriber's right to use the system in a manner privately beneficial and not publicly harmful. Serious competition to equipment furnished by the telephone company did not develop at that time as modified tariffs continued to prohibit connection of privately provided devices. In March 1968, a decade after the *Hush-A-Phone* decision, the telephone companies advised customers that use of the Carterfone to connect privately owned mobile radio systems with the telephone system was a tariff violation. In 1968 the FCC ruled that the telephone company tariffs were unlawful because they prevented connection of a device that improved the utility of the service and did not adversely affect the telephone system's operation or the system's utility for others. The telephone companies did not appeal. Rather, they modified their tariffs to permit connection if telephone company connection arrangements and network control signaling units were used to protect the network from technical harm. By 1975, 446,000 protective connecting arrangements had been installed.

Following the *Carterfone* decision, suppliers began to market PBXs (private branch exchanges) and key systems. Mebane Home Telephone Company, a small independent company in North Carolina, sought exemption from allowing connection of customer-furnished PBXs and key systems. The firm claimed it would suffer economic harm if equipment revenues were diverted to other suppliers. It also argued that the *Carterfone* decision dealt with connection of different terminal equipment and not with replacement of any part of the telephone system. In 1975 the FCC ruled that telephone users could replace telephone company terminal equipment with equipment made by other manufacturers.

In 1972 the FCC initiated a federal-state joint board proceeding on connection of terminal equipment not provided by the phone company. Suppliers of non-Bell equipment claimed that, if customers had to pay for special protective devices in addition to the cost of non-Bell terminal equipment, the overall cost would exceed the cost of using standard Bell terminal equipment and would benefit Bell financially. The board recommended that users should not have to obtain protective interconnecting arrangements from the phone company to use terminal equipment from other makers, if that equipment contained appropriate protective circuitry and was registered with the FCC.

However, before action was completed in that proceeding, two state regulatory authorities issued decisions to prevent connection of customer-provided terminal equipment to the lines of telephone companies operating in those states. A trade association petitioned the FCC to determine to what extent its ruling had preempted state action. The FCC ruled that it had exclusive authority. That decision, in the case of the *Telerent Leasing Corporation,* was sustained by the U.S. Court of Appeals in 1976; the Supreme Court declined review. The FCC then established a terminal equipment registration program.

More recently the telephone companies have sought to require all single-line users to rent at least one telephone-company telephone (primary instrument) to facilitate testing and to maintain the integrity of the telephone network. The telephone companies contend that subscribers who provide their own equipment often call the telephone company for help when the problem lies with the terminal equipment furnished by the subscribers, thus increasing costs which must be borne by others. The primary instrument concept was rejected by the FCC, which felt that subscribers would adequately maintain the terminal equipment that they supplied and that competition would permit innovation and meet the varying demands of users. Today there is significant competition for the supply of terminal equipment for telephone users.

**Specialized Common Carriers.** Before the 1960s, only the telephone companies and Western Union offered private line services—that is, point-to-point communications facilities dedicated to a single user, often to provide capabilities not available through standard telephone lines.[26] In the 1950s, the Bell System used coaxial cable to provide the greater capacity needed for private line television signal relay. Cable television systems also required private lines to relay television signals to remote areas where signals could not be taken off the air satisfactorily. Microwave radio technology could also provide the greater carrying capacity needed for such services, so-called broadband service, more economically than coaxial cable because cable required the phone companies to obtain extensive right-of-way privileges from private property holders. The Bell System adopted microwave transmission for television signal relay services.

The most efficient transfer of data from computers, using digital rather than analog signals, also required broadband capacity through either coaxial cables or microwave radio. Large businesses sought to establish their own communications systems, either to cover remote areas or to save the cost of renting facilities.

In its 1959 *Above 890* decision, the FCC examined a number of issues concerning the use of microwave systems by private businesses. The telephone companies argued that a proliferation of separate private line facilities would be inefficient and contrary to the public interest. The FCC concluded, however, that enough frequencies were available in the microwave range to accommodate the future needs of both common carrier and private microwave systems. It found that allowing private microwave systems would not affect the ability of the common carriers to provide service to the general public and ruled that private systems which meet proper technical standards would be authorized to operate, even though common carrier facilities could provide the same service. Although private line services accounted for only a small part of the Bell System's total revenues, the potential for growth in such earnings was tremendous. By 1975 nearly 600 private microwave systems were in operation.

In 1969 the FCC authorized Microwave Communications, Inc. (MCI), as a specialized common carrier, to provide private line microwave service between Chicago and St. Louis. The FCC found that competition was reasonably feasible and the system could be expected to benefit the public. By May 1976, 214 applications had been filed with the FCC to construct microwave facilities and provide specialized common carrier service to various parts of the country.

In its 1971 *Specialized Common Carriers* decision the FCC established a policy favoring new entry into the specialized communications field. The FCC then felt that new markets developed through such entry would cover only limited geographic areas and that the specialized common carriers would be unlikely to construct facilities on a nationwide basis at one time in competition with the established carriers. Thus, AT&T would not lose revenues to the extent claimed by AT&T. The FCC ordered the phone companies to permit new carriers to connect with their interstate telephone facilities on a reasonable and nondiscriminatory basis.

The FCC recognized that the established carriers should be allowed to depart from uniform nationwide averaging of rates for private lines services in competing with the new specialized carriers. In subsequent decisions affecting rates, the FCC has sought to prevent the Bell System from subsidizing its private lines offerings by using earnings on monopoly services. However, FCC Chairman Wiley has acknowledged that existing telephone company accounting systems are not adequate for today's regulatory problems.

In 1972 in its *Domsat* decision, the FCC extended this private lines multiple entry policy to permit the use of domestic communications satellites by domestic satellite carriers in addition to the Communications Satellite Corporation (COMSAT), which Congress had given a monopoly for international satellite communications. The commission sought to "handicap" Bell System competition by delaying AT&T's use of satellite systems for private lines services for three years.

Beginning in 1973, the FCC authorized value-added networks (VANs) to provide private lines communications services. Typically a VAN leases lines from established carriers and provides specialized services, such as packet switching, to data communications concerns over and above the basic transmission service, so-called value added services.[27] Common carrier tariffs generally prohibited simple resale of leased line services and prevented users from pooling their needs and sharing a line. In 1976, the FCC adopted a policy of unlimited sharing and resale of common carrier private lines facilities and services.

In 1974, MCI and affiliated carriers filed revisions to their tariff covering interstate services to establish rates for a class of metered-use telephone service known as Execunet. A local subscriber could use this service from any telephone in the user's city by dialing a local MCI telephone number, then an access code, and then any regular telephone number in a distant city. Customers were billed on a time and distance basis subject to a monthly minimum. The FCC and AT&T viewed Execunet as more than a point-to-point private line service. They saw it as so like AT&T's message telecommunications service (MTS) that it was essentially a switched public message telephone service that encroached on what the FCC and AT&T regarded as the authorized monopoly position of the established telephone companies over other than private line telephone services. The FCC concluded that Execunet service had not been authorized. However, the Court of Appeals ruled that, under the Communications Act of 1934, once a carrier had been licensed it is free to initiate and implement new rates and services that can be provided over existing communications lines until the FCC, after hearings, determines the action to be unlawful. The court acknowledged that the FCC can impose conditions on the initial issuance of licenses that require advance FCC approval of new service offerings, but the FCC had not done this in the case of MCI. In any event, the court found that the FCC would have to make an affirmative determination that "the public convenience and necessity" require such conditions. The court concluded, moreover, that the FCC had not to that time determined that the public interest would be served by creating a monopoly for AT&T in the MTS field.[28]

The FCC then commenced a proceeding to determine whether long distance telephone service should be a monopoly service. That proceeding is still pending. In May 1979, the FCC proposed the elimination of rate filings by all but dominant carriers, that is, those whose market position might enable them to earn excessive amounts. If such action is taken, the Bell System would be subject to rate regulation but specialized carriers would not.[29]

**Data Processing by Communications Common Carriers.** In 1973 the FCC concluded a seven-year inquiry into the types of computer services that it might regulate. The FCC was concerned that communications common carriers could cross-subsidize their computer services and thus compete unfairly. The FCC then concluded that a service that combined data processing and message switching would be classified as a "hybrid communication service" and regulated by the FCC if the data processing capability were incidental to the message-switching function. If the computer service were more prominent than message switching, the service would be classified as the "hybrid computer service." The Bell System was prohibited from offering data processing services either directly or indirectly. However, other communications common carriers could furnish data processing services through a separate subsidiary under restrictions included in federal regulations.[30]

Application of the concept of hybrid services has proved difficult. In 1976, the FCC initiated a second inquiry to determine whether a new definition of terms in the computer field was required. More recently, the FCC has tentatively decided to classify data services as incidental to communication services and to permit AT&T and its competitors to offer such services either on an unregulated basis or by filing tariffs subject to FCC regulation.[31]

**Telegraph Services.** In January 1979, the FCC ended Western Union's monopoly in telegraph message service and approved the application of Graphnet Systems, Inc., to become Western Union's first competitor. This action is expected to affect services that produced approximately $95 million in annual revenues. The FCC decision would also permit Western Union to drop service to unprofitable areas which it has previously served because of its monopoly position as a common carrier.[32]

## Antitrust Enforcement Suits

AT&T owns a majority of stock in twenty-three of the twenty-five Bell operating companies. The Western Electric company (an unregulated manufacturing and supply company) is wholly owned by AT&T, and Bell Telephone Laboratories, the research arm of the Bell System, is owned jointly by AT&T and Western Electric. In 1939, after a study of the structure of the Bell System, the FCC concluded that Bell was properly structured in the light of the technology of the industry. In 1949 the Department of Justice brought a suit to break up the Bell System. This suit was settled in 1956 by a consent agreement that left intact the structure of the Bell System but restricted the system essentially to regulated common carrier activities. (See in this connection the section "Fairness in Competition" below.)

Communications law reform legislation introduced in the 95th Congress would have required AT&T to divest itself of the Western Electric Company. That provision has been omitted from the bills currently pending, but the question of whether the restrictions imposed by the 1956 consent decree should be lifted or retained is very much alive. In addition, key members of Congress realize that the Justice Department filed an antitrust suit against AT&T, the Western Electric Company, and Bell Telephone Laboratories in 1974. That suit is awaiting trial. Senator Howard M. Metzenbaum (D-Ohio) has stated that congressional action on the pending bills should not be construed as obviating the need for structural reform of the Bell System requested in the pending suit.[33] This analysis will not comment on the merits of the pending litigation, but the positions of the litigants in that suit are summarized as background for the discussion of communications issues that follows.

The suit filed by the Justice Department charges that the Bell System is locked together by formal and informal means so that AT&T can orchestrate policies and conduct for the system and that AT&T in fact exercises centralized control. The suit claims that Bell uses the regulatory process to resist and delay the entry of competitors and to maintain its monopoly position. When entry of competitors is authorized, the suit charges, Bell refuses to deal with the new entrant such as in providing interconnections for private line traffic. If negotiations for interconnection are undertaken, it is asserted, Bell may stonewall the negotiations to delay effective competition.

In the meantime, it is claimed, Bell tries to catch up with the competition by developing comparable equipment, and Bell may preannounce new equipment or services to discourage customers from contracting with Bell's competitors. Bell companies, it is asserted, acquire equipment and supplies from Western Electric to the greatest extent possible and seek to discourage other suppliers who need Bell business to make significant penetration in the communications supply market.

The Justice Department cites in detail a series of Bell offerings and activities to support its claim that the defendants have violated the Sherman Antitrust Act. It claims that its evidence will show extension of monopoly power to other markets, pricing abuses, customer leasing requirements, reciprocity, tracking and surveillance of competitors, vertical integration of the Bell System, abuse of the regulatory process, and agreements for dividing markets. The suit asks that ownership of interstate facilities be separated from ownership of local communications facilities and that provision of communications services be separated from the manufacturing and the research and development functions.[34]

The defendants contend that competition in an earlier era was brought to an end by government policy as communications carriers were subjected to public utility regulation. Regulatory authorities were the ones, it is claimed, who fostered telephone rates favoring residential consumers; these authorities have insisted on depreciation policies for company assets appropriate for regulated utilities in a monopoly environment but unsuitable for meeting new competitors in solid competition.

Defendants contend that when the FCC authorized competition by specialized carriers, it deferred the establishment of principles for competitive rate making just as it had avoided defining the scope, price, terms, and conditions of interconnection. Thus, it is asserted, the Bell companies were required to respond to competition without appropriate guidance from the regulatory authorities. Intercity private lines rates were deaveraged, for example, to bring prices of services more in line with cost and to mitigate the cream skimming of competitors.

The defendants claim that no divestiture is needed because Congress investigated the structure of the Bell System in 1932 and left industry structure unchanged. The FCC investigated industry structure, and its administrative law judge rejected divestiture. The defendents argue that Bell has created a mechanism to stimulate greater purchases of equipment and supplies from outside sources and that, in any event, regulatory authorities review the prices paid by Bell for Western Electric equipment and supplies, so there is no opportunity for overcharge.

The defendants deny monopoly power in any of the markets the Justice Department claims they have monopolized, and they respond to charges about specific events and service offerings by arguing that Bell conduct was a reasonable response to competitive forces under the circumstances involved. They assert that the Supreme Court has sustained the right of vigorous participation in regulatory proceedings; that Bell's participation has been honest, reasonable, and responsible; but, in any event, Bell has suffered from manipulation of the regulatory process by others.[35]

# 3

## Pending Legislative Proposals

### H.R. 3333

Representatives Lionel Van Deerlin (D-Calif.), James M. Collins (R-Tex.), and James T. Broyhill (R-N.C.) have introduced H.R. 3333 to revise the communications laws, a bill that would make major changes in the way we regulate communications activities. The provisions of this bill affecting the regulation of broadcast activities have been abandoned by Representative Van Deerlin, the communications subcommittee chairman; this analysis will deal only with the nonbroadcast aspects of the bill.

In general, H.R. 3333 would rely on competition in preference to government regulation, except to the extent marketplace forces fail to protect the public interest. The bill does not define the term "public interest" and the term "common carrier" is not used. The bill tries to make sure that everyone would still have access to telephone service, but it would allow firms to leave the telecommunications market as well as to enter it.

Computer and information services would be deregulated. The provision of terminal equipment would not be subject to state or federal regulation, except to make sure it complies with federal technical standards. Shared use of telecommunications services and facilities on a nonprofit basis would not be regulated. Cable systems would be free of federal and state regulation, except that pole attachments would be subject to federal regulation if they are not regulated by the states.

Cable companies could compete fully with telephone companies in all areas, including the provision of basic voice service. Such companies could also provide incidental services such as burglar alarms, fire alarms, and data transmission.

In domestic telecommunications, only dominant carriers (the Bell System and perhaps Western Union) would be regulated and then only for a period of ten years. Federal jurisdiction would be determined primarily on the basis of "interexchange" (intercity) activities. States would only regulate basic voice telephone service at the local level. Only dominant carriers engaged in interexchange services would have to file tariffs at the federal level. No restrictions are placed on the entry of new carriers in any telecommunications market.

A new and less powerful five-member Communications Regulatory Commission (CRC) would replace the FCC, and administrative procedures would be streamlined. The dominant carrier would have the burden of showing that a rate is just and reasonable, but, if the CRC determines that the market involved is substantially competitive, those who challenge the rate would have the burden of showing that it is unjust or unreasonable.

The traditional fully distributed cost method used in calculating regulated carriers' financial needs, under which the carrier must allocate a portion of its historical or embedded costs to any new service, would be scrapped and costs would be assigned on a prospective cost basis. Depreciation rates for the regulated carriers would be based on economic efficiency and not simply on the physical life of assets. CRC would be required to develop a long-run marginal cost methodology for submission to the Congress.

The bill would override restraints placed on AT&T and the Western Electric Company by the 1956 antitrust consent decree, and would permit the Bell System to provide unregulated services. However, AT&T and its affiliated companies would have to deal with each other at arm's length and offer products, services, or facilities to other companies on the same terms as they offer them to members of the Bell System.

The bill would not require AT&T to divest itself of Western Electric. Carriers could meet (on notice to the attorney general with opportunity for his representative to attend) to plan, construct, and maintain the nationwide core network and establish through rates.

Separations procedures would be eliminated, but local telephone companies would be allowed to collect an access charge regulated by state authorities to ensure that all interexchange service carriers make a fair contribution to maintaining low-cost local telephone service. However, this subsidy would be phased out over a ten-year period, and no provision is made for its replacement. Domestic carriers in the interexchange market could charge for their services but they could not discriminate as to rates and conditions of service.

A National Telecommunications Agency, replacing the National Telecommunications and Information Administration in the Department of Commerce, would be established in the executive branch to develop and implement national telecommunications policy.

## H.R. 1580

Representative Jack Edwards (R-Ala.) has introduced H.R. 1580 to reaffirm the intent of Congress with respect to the structure of the common carrier telecommunications industry and for other purposes. This bill is a partial restatement of the so-called Bell bill, introduced by approximately 200 members of Congress in the 95th Congress.

Section 1 states that the technical integrity of a nationwide telecommunications system and its coordinated planning, design, operation, and maintenance are indispensable elements of an interstate communications network and necessary to promote universal service of high quality at reasonable charges. This section also finds that all companies providing common carrier telecommunications services should be subject to the same regulatory process, although small independent companies operating exclusively within a state should be excluded from federal jurisdiction.

Section 2 would amend Section 201(b) of the Communications Act of 1934 to define "compensatory charge" for a service as one that equals or exceeds the cost of the additional facilities required to provide the service. The FCC could not hold a compensatory charge up to a particular level to protect traffic or revenues from a service offered or provided by another carrier.

Section 3 would amend Section 2(b) of the 1934 act to limit FCC jurisdiction over terminal or station equipment and so forth, even that used for both intrastate and for interstate or foreign communications services. The FCC could regulate such equipment only to ensure the technical integrity and capacity of a coordinated nationwide telephone network. If, after holding an evidentiary hearing on the record, the FCC found that such regulation was needed, it would have exclusive jurisdiction and could issue regulations relating to use or connection.

Section 4 would amend Section 3 of the 1934 act to define "intrastate communications service" as any service that provides intrastate communication and to reiterate state jurisdiction over terminal equipment and facilities as in Section 3.

Section 5 would add a new Section 224 to the act defining certain terms and providing that the FCC shall not authorize construction, operation, or acquisition of any communication or transmission line by any specialized carrier that proposes to furnish interstate communications service or the extension, modification, or renewal of a license or permit of such a carrier, or the operation of any telephone or telegraph common carrier unless, after it holds an evidentiary hearing on the record, it finds that such is required by present or future public convenience and necessity and will not impair the technical integrity and capacity for a coordinated nationwide telephone network.

## S. 611

Senators Ernest F. Hollings (D-S.C.), Howard W. Cannon (D-Nev.), and Ted Stevens (R-Alas.) introduced S. 611 to amend the Communications Act of 1934 in significant respects. The nonbroadcast features of the bill include the following.

The universal service goal of the 1934 act would be retained, but a new goal would be added, promoting full and fair competition in the provision of equipment and services to the maximum extent feasible and consistent with the act.

As in H.R. 3333, the term "common carrier" would not be used. Local exchange areas having a community of interests and which could be larger than a single exchange would be set by state authorities. Communications between such exchange areas—that is, interexchange telecommunications—would be subject to FCC regulation. However, the bill would establish a rebuttable presumption that there are no basic technological, operational, or economic barriers to effective competition in the provision of interexchange telecommunications service.

The degree of regulation to which a carrier would be subject would depend in part on whether it is classified either as a "Category 1" or a "Category 2" carrier. This classification would be based on the degree of effective competition to which the carrier is subject, its dominance in its own service market or markets, and the extent to which its service is essential to the public. Markets would be classified on four bases as an aid in classifying carriers.

Category 2 carriers would be those that either are not subject to effective competition for any type or class of service or provide essential services that cannot be left to competition. A carrier that earns no more than a third of its revenues from a particular market would be presumed to be subject to effective competition until the contrary is shown, but a carrier providing a new service for less than two years would not be designated as a Category 2 carrier solely because it is not subject to effective competition.

Category 1 carriers would be subject to no restrictions other than the reporting of information that would let the FCC monitor the market and determine whether the carriers should be reclassified. Category 2 carriers could be regulated as to rates, construction permits, and so forth as at present and also as to switching equipment, which is not specifically regulated under current law. They could not freely exit from the provision of a service as under H.R. 3333. The FCC would be required to lower the level of regulation for a Category 2 carrier as competition develops and the need for supervision declines.

S. 611 distinguishes between the provision of communications services—which may be subject to regulation—and information services, telecommunications equipment, and information software—which would not be regulated. Companies which provide only hardware would be unregulated, though the FCC could establish and enforce standards for terminal equipment.

Category 2 carriers would include AT&T and any other carrier that provides an interexchange service for which it is not subject to effective competition. Under certain conditions, a Category 2 carrier could sell or lease information services, telecommunications or electronic equipment, or information software. It could also enter service markets where the other carriers are Category 1 carriers. However, the carrier could do those things only if (1) it forms a fully separate subsidiary that deals with the parent carrier at arm's length, or (2) the FCC, after a hearing, sets accounting or structural safeguards to protect customers of rate-regulated services and to protect the competitiveness of the market.

In lieu of separations and settlements, local exchange companies would collect access charges from interexchange carriers, such as MCI or AT&T's Long Lines Department, for connection with the exchange's facilities. Access charges would be based on only indentifiable costs and would be regulated by the FCC. The portion of separations and settlements now representing nonallocable costs and subsidy would be superseded by a pool financed by a surcharge on interexchange traffic. The pool would be administered by a federal-state joint board. Funds from the pool would be used for a basic exchange maintenance program; allocations would be determined by relative use of an exchange's facilities for interexchange as compared with local traffic. A supplemental allocation would be made to small companies with less than thirty subscribers per route mile to assure the viability of small rural systems.

Rural telecommunications services would also be promoted through federal assistance to state planning, extension of Rural Electrification Administration (REA) assistance to nontelephone carriers, and FCC revision of rules which impede development of rural telecommunications systems.

Category 2 carriers that are not subject to effective competition would have to provide interconnection with any other carrier on request for an agreed charge; if the two carriers could not reach agreement, the FCC would set a reasonable charge after a hearing. Tariffs filed by Category 2 carriers not subject to effective competition would not be effective until the FCC conditionally accepts or finally approves them; the FCC would have the authority to prescribe a fair tariff, in addition to its authority to accept or reject the proposed tariff. An expedited FCC procedure would apply to tariffs filed by Category 2 carriers that are subject to effective competition. A Category 2 carrier could choose to file a long-term facilities construction plan; if this were approved, the carrier would not have to seek a separate certification before it could start on each item in the plan.

Regulation of cable systems, other than for broadcast retransmission, would be the same as for other nonbroadcast telecommunications carriers. However, if the state chooses, the cable local exchange area need not match the telephone local exchange area. Interconnection with local cable facilities by interexchange carriers would be regulated by the FCC; local matters that do not involve broadcast signal retransmission rules of the FCC would be regulated by state or local authorities, if at all. Utility pole owners would be required to permit pole attachments by cable systems, including cooperatives, on a reasonable basis.

## S. 622

Senators Barry Goldwater (R-Ariz.), Harrison H. Schmitt (R-N.Mex.), and Larry Pressler (R-S.Dak.) have introduced S. 622 to amend the Communications Act of 1934 to develop marketplace competition in the provision of certain services and to provide for deregulation of those services.

A new Section 225 would be added to the 1934 act for the stated purposes, among others, of promoting marketplace competition as soon as possible, ensuring universal voice-grade telephone service, maximizing available services, and preventing predatory and anticompetitive practices. Regulation would be phased out over a six-year period by the issuance and implementation of FCC regulations. However, voice-grade telephone service would be offered and provided as a regulated monopoly in local telephone exchanges until state commissions determine that competition will maintain reasonable rates and promote improved service through new technologies. Boundaries of a local telephone exchange would be set by state authorities.

The FCC would have jurisdiction over all interexchange telecommunications services provided by common carriers. Any subscriber could connect terminal equipment of his own choice, subject to technical standards established by the FCC. FCC regulation would establish a transition plan and classify common carriers according to the degree of regulation needed by each. A common carrier could offer any telecommunications service notwithstanding its classification by the FCC if it is reasonably qualified financially, if it is not owned or controlled by "foreign interests," and if there are no anticompetitive elements in the provision of proposed services. Both monopoly and nonmonopoly services could be provided by the same carrier, but one service could not cross-subsidize the other. The FCC would prescribe an accounting system to separately state revenues and costs attributable to monopoly and nonmonopoly services, to determine the appropriate access charge for interconnection with a local exchange, and so forth. FCC regulations would also specify when common carriers that supply monopoly services must form subsidiaries to perform certain services.

An access compensation charge would be paid by common carriers interconnecting with the facilities of local exchanges. Sums from the resulting compensation fund would be distributed to provide for actual costs of interconnection; if necessary, additional sums would be paid to maintain reasonable customer rates for basic voice-grade telephone service. This procedure and charge would be phased out in six years.

Regulations would provide for accelerated equipment depreciation rates; the FCC would oversee these rates during the six-year period. The FCC would ensure that rates and charges for telecommunications services, other than for monopoly services, would be increased no more than 5 percent or reduced by no more than 10 percent for a period of two years; during the next four years, rates for such services could not be increased more than 10 percent nor reduced by more than 20 percent. Rates would be effective on ninety days' notice to the FCC and the public, subject to FCC investigation and rejection.

The FCC would provide a procedure to ensure interconnection of common carriers providing telephone toll service with one another and with the facilities of local exchanges. It would help form and oversee an association of common carriers to manage the facilities providing toll services and interconnection with local exchanges. Such carriers would be allowed to meet and agree, with FCC oversight, on matters affecting the design plan, maintenance of telephone toll facilities, and development of interconnection standards.

Common carrier proposals to offer nonmonopoly telecommunications services and to construct or expand facilities would be automatically authorized unless the FCC determines within ninety days that a substantial and material question of fact exists as to whether the investment is in the public interest.

Telephone toll service could not be reduced, discontinued, or impaired by a common carrier unless the FCC determines this to be in the public interest. The FCC would adjust the level of regulation under its transition plan to remove marketplace deficiencies, anticompetitive behavior, and other practices that frustrate the purposes of the section. The FCC would provide a continuous review to ensure that nationwide telephone toll services exist through marketplace competition and make appropriate reports.

A new Section 335 to the 1934 act finds that cable systems are engaged in interstate commerce and would subject them to federal regulation. Federal rules would take precedence over state rules as to technical standards for system and equipment compatibility, including the interoperability of cable systems, subscriber attachment of receiving or terminal equipment, and certain provisions applicable to broadcast activities. States and their instrumentalities could regulate cable systems to the extent their regulations are not inconsistent with the grant of federal authority.

## H.R. 6121

On December 13, 1979, Representative Van Deerlin and fourteen cosponsors introduced the Telecommunications Act of 1979. This bill would amend the 1934 act as it relates to nonbroadcast domestic telecommunications. It does not attempt complete revision of the 1934 act as did its predecessor, H.R. 3333. Both bills seek the deregulation of nonbroadcast domestic telecommunications, but H.R. 6121 sets no time limit for achieving deregulation. The FCC would not be replaced as in H.R. 3333, but a transitional joint board would be created for a period of forty-five months to move domestic telecommunications toward deregulation by reducing the subsidy of local telephone services, enforcing accounting standards to disclose cross subsidies, and so forth. The board, and the FCC following the board's expiration, would allocate a portion of the access charges imposed on interexchange carriers for interconnection with intraexchange facilities to a national telecommunications pool or fund from which it would disburse money to ensure basic telecommunications services at reasonable and affordable rates, if market forces are unable to achieve this objective, and to maintain reasonable access to interexchange telecommunications facilities. Terminal equipment and devices would be unregulated except for technical standards set by the FCC. States would set the boundaries of intraexchange areas, and they would set the amount of interexchange access fees if the FCC delegates this responsibility to them under standards set by the transitional joint board. All carriers would be subject to federal regulation to the extent required to address national defense and emergency preparedness needs, and to ensure basic interexchange service at reasonable and affordable rates upon reasonable request and without discrimination as to rates or conditions of service. Basic telecommunications service is defined to mean basic two-way switched voice telephone service, but the FCC could expand this definition to include other telecommunications services.

H.R. 6121 would regulate dominant carriers, that is, those that furnish telecommunications services or facilities in a substantial percentage of the markets or submarkets for interexchange services and that have the ability in a substantial percentage of such markets or submarkets to raise or lower prices without significantly raising or lowering customer reliance on their services, because of the absence of comparable alternative services or facilities. Even dominant carriers could offer nonbasic interexchange services without regulation if such services are provided through a fully separated subsidiary as defined under strict guidelines set in the bill and if the carriers have accounting systems adequate to prevent cross subsidy of services. A grandfather provision would require a dominant carrier to obtain a certificate from the FCC that discontinuance of or deregulation of a service offered on the date of enactment of the bill would not be contrary to public convenience and necessity. However, the FCC could reassert regulatory jurisdiction over such services if effective competition ceases or if regulation is necessary to serve the public convenience and necessity. The FCC or the person petitioning for renewal of regulatory authority in such cases would have the burden of proof.

H.R. 6121 would affirm FCC authority to define services, facilities, and products that are incidental to telecommunications in disputed cases. AT&T and its affiliates could offer unregulated services, facilities, and products, and it could offer services, facilities, and products incidental to telecommunications, including data processing and the manufacture, sale, and lease of telephone equipment and terminal devices, notwithstanding the 1956 antitrust consent decree, through a fully separated subsidiary subject to required accounting procedures. Carriers could meet on notice to the FCC to design, plan, construct, and maintain telecommunications networks and facilities, develop technical standards, and agree on tariffs for joint or through services. If competing carriers attend, they would have to furnish a transcript of the proceedings to the FCC for public availability. The bill disclaims any attempt to influence the outcome of pending antitrust litigation or the application of the antitrust laws. The FCC's authority to regulate cable TV provided by intraexchange carriers would be continued.

Senators who have submitted bills may introduce refined versions of their proposals. As this is written these revised bills have not been introduced. A presidential message of October 31, 1979, however, outlines in broad terms the administration's support for the principle of deregulation of the nonbroadcast telecommunications industry.[36] The administration will not present a bill of its own, but the changes it endorses include the following:

• Congress should give the FCC explicit authority to forbear from regulation when the public is clearly protected from the abuse of market power, since the FCC's power to forbear is in dispute. The administration proposes that Congress preclude regulation by the FCC when a firm lacks market power or when a dominant firm is offering services in an area with effective competition and when there is assurance against anticompetitive behavior, such as through use of a fully separated subsidiary. The FCC should have authority to reestablish regulation if conditions require this, according to the administration.

• The administration suggests that the relationship between long lines activities and local operating companies could be left to the FCC for resolution under existing authority and in the light of prevailing competitive conditions. It would leave the relationships involving Western Electric Company, Bell Telephone Laboratories, and the remaining Bell companies to the FCC, with the caveats that the operating companies be required to open up a substantial part of their equipment procurement to competition and that the FCC should be encouraged to complete the pending proceeding involving these issues by a certain date.

• Any legislation, in the administration's view, should be neutral as to pending antitrust suits and future litigation, but Congress should allow AT&T to engage in unregulated telecommunications and incidental activities, such as computerized data processing, notwithstanding the 1956 antitrust consent decree which restricts AT&T activities.

• Because of AT&T's size and wealth, the administration would bar the corporation from programming mass media services to inform the electorate on issues of public concern.

• The separations and settlements procedures that provide a subsidy to the local exchanges should be phased out in favor of a nondiscriminatory access charge to long distance carriers for local costs associated with originating and terminating intercity services. The administration would leave such matters to the FCC after a three-year transition period.

• If rate deaveraging or other factors produce high costs in unique situations, the administration would protect continued provision of universal telephone service by direct subsidies.

• Like most of the pending bills, the administration proposes a reallocation of federal jurisdiction that would encompass long distance (interexchange) services while leaving jurisdiction over the local exchanges to state authorities.

The discussion draft of a revised S. 622 that may be introduced by Senators Goldwater, Schmitt, Pressler, and Ted Stevens (R-Alas.) would modify S. 622 by eliminating the firm six-year period for completion of deregulation, and it would make a number of other changes. Local distribution facilities employed to provide interexchange services would be subject to federal regulation, but the provision of terminal equipment would be deregulated over a three-year period and neither the FCC nor state authorities would have jurisdiction thereafter, except for the FCC's prescription of minimum standards for equipment to be interconnected with the telephone network. Resale and sharing of telecommunications services would be completely deregulated. The acquisition, processing, or marketing of information or program materials from computers would be excluded from the definition of telecommunications services. The principal criterion for the classification of communications carriers as to the extent of regulation required would be the extent to which the carrier could raise or lower prices without significant effect on the amount of services demanded by customers. Analysis of the costs and benefits to customers would determine when certain services would have to be provided through a fully separated affiliate.

A provision, apparently aimed at freeing AT&T from the restrictions of the 1956 antitrust decree, would permit any carrier (or its affiliate in certain cases) to offer any unregulated service or product notwithstanding any judicial decree or any FCC classification of the carrier, if the offering is not otherwise prohibited by law. The provision in S. 622 calling for the FCC to oversee the establishment of an association of carriers to manage the telephone network is omitted from the discussion draft. Access charges for interconnection by an interexchange carrier with a local or intraexchange carrier would be handled somewhat differently in the discussion draft. The portion of an access charge reflecting joint and common costs associated with local distribution of interexchange services and all costs that vary directly with the service provided would be paid directly to the intraexchange carrier. A contribution from the interexchange carrier to maintain reasonable local exchange service rates would be paid into an access compensation fund and a joint transition board would make payments from that fund to subsidize local exchanges. The provision in S. 622 that would require elimination of the access charge in six years is omitted from the discussion draft. Specific provision would be made for special funding to aid rural telecommunications services and extensive provisions are included in the discussion draft to protect the privacy of carriers' customers. Any cable system franchise fee set by state or local authorities would be limited to no more than 5 percent of a system's annual revenues.

# 4

## Issues and Arguments

### Regulated Monopoly versus Competition

The goals of pending legislative proposals range from the reaffirmation of the universal service goal of the Communications Act of 1934 and a return to the provision of service by monopoly carriers, on the one hand, to opening all aspects of nonbroadcast telecommunications to competition and drastically reducing the level of regulation, on the other hand.

In pioneer days, monopoly franchises were given to some business enterprises as a means of ensuring services needed to open and develop the frontier. In more modern times, legislative bodies have provided for regulated monopolies when they believed that certain services could be provided more conveniently and efficiently by such monopolies. Regulation has frequently been used, when market forces are deficient, in preference to government ownership—gas and electric utilities are examples. Regulation has been found necessary to compensate, in some instances, for the inability of competition to provide adequate regulation.[37]

Proponents of deregulation and competition contend that in proper circumstances competition will allocate resources to make the maximum contribution to total output, produce prices which reflect marginal costs (the added cost of producing the last unit sold), bring to consumers the goods or services they want at prices they are willing to pay, and pay producers their costs of production plus a reasonable profit. Regulation, they contend, cannot duplicate this complex interactive process unless a government agency intervenes in every detail of the activity involved.[38]

Proponents of deregulation believe that advances in technology and its applications make competition practical and that competition is necessary to give the public the full benefit of these innovations. The established telephone companies contend that significant social goals can best be met through perpetuation of a regulated monopoly and the current system of cross subsidies for local exchanges and certain services through rate averaging and through the separation process.

This section will examine the arguments for and against deregulation and competition in the context of the principal goals emphasized by the participants in the current debate over telecommunications policy. The principal differences between proponents and opponents of deregulation and competition involve the means recommended to achieve stated goals rather than the goals themselves.

**Universal Service.** In the Communications Act of 1934, Congress stated that the purpose of the regulation provided by that act was to make nationwide and worldwide service available to *all* Americans. None of the pending bills would abandon the goal of universal service, though some of the bills advance other goals related to quality of service and to innovation.[39]

When the 1934 act was adopted, only 31 percent of the households in the United States had telephone service. Now 94.5 percent have such service. Most observers agree that universal service has been substantially realized, but there is disagreement as to the effect deregulation and competition will have on preserving the gains that have been made and extending service to still other households. Edward P. Larkin, a member of the New York Public Service Commission, claims that universal service could not have been attained without a telephone monopoly.[40] Larkin and witnesses for the established telephone companies assert that basic telecommunications service for the masses has been achieved through cross subsidies from rate averaging and the separations process. (See the section "Pricing Policies" above and the subsection "Affordable Rates and Equity" below.)

According to James E. Olson, vice chairman of AT&T, the two keys to preserving and extending universal service are (1) the integrated nationwide public switched telephone network, through which the telephone companies jointly offer services under common tariffs, and (2) the economic incentive system presented by the settlements process discussed in the section "Pricing Policies." In Olson's view, the operating phone companies could not afford to invest in facilities needed for the support of the nationwide network if the settlements system did not make up for revenues these companies are unable to generate locally and encourage timely investment in capital assets to ensure optimum network performance. With support from the settlements system telephone operating companies are willing to invest in improving nationwide service even though these investments would not generate new revenues for them directly or tangibly improve local service.[41]

The established telephone companies insist that the deregulation bills underestimate the importance and complexity of the joint engineering and operational planning needed to provide quality telephone service in every community in the nation. (See the subsection "Innovation and Quality of Service" below.) Separations revenues are referred to as the glue that binds the telephone companies together. If separations are abolished as proposed, it is argued that the incentive to make investments to benefit the network as a whole will be lost, and operating companies will look only to their own costs and the profits they can generate locally.

The established telephone companies operate as regulated monopolies. Telephone company witnesses note that as common carriers providing regulated monopoly services they are required to act in the public interest. They are required to furnish service on reasonable request, consistent with the universal service mandate, and they are barred by law from unjust or unreasonable discrimination. Communications lines cannot be built or extended without a certificate of public convenience and necessity from the appropriate regulatory authorities and, a corollary of the foregoing, service cannot be impaired or abandoned contrary to the public convenience and necessity.

Phone company witnesses assert that some of the bills would depart so far from the public interest concept that the term "common carrier" would no longer be used in the basic federal law that governs the provision of telecommunications services. The administration's top spokesman on telecommunications matters acknowledges that in the competitive marketplace contemplated a carrier should not be forced to provide unprofitable service and that freedom of exit from a market or service is a corollary of freedom of entry.[42] In the view of the established telephone companies, universal service cannot be taken for granted if competition replaces regulated monopoly. Competitors will concentrate on the profitable markets and services and ignore the goal of universal service. Such cream skimming will force the established telephone companies to meet competition by deaveraging interexchange rates for both intrastate and interstate calls—that is, by charging on the basis of the actual costs rather than by averaging rates to promote universal service. Bell System Long Lines may need access charges that do not subsidize local telephone services, if they are to compete effectively with specialized carriers. Such a change can only mean, according to the established telephone companies, that a great many telephone users will have to pay substantially more for telephone service. Those who will be hardest hit are low-income households, those least able to afford telephone service. Deregulation of telecommunications with carrier right of exit as well as entry could mean loss of service to certain areas. Bell spokesmen conclude that new entrants should be required to show that the public convenience and necessity would be served by their entry and that competitors should not be allowed to enter if Bell service is currently adequate.

Advocates of deregulation and competition deny that the actions they recommend would reduce the percentage of households with basic telephone service or prevent additional gains.[43] They note that the statements of purpose in the pending bills support universal service and that H.R. 3333 would permit states to establish an access compensation charge high enough to subsidize local operating companies during a transition period and allow state regulatory commissions to pool a portion of the access charges for distribution to local exchanges in a manner consistent with rules and procedures of such commissions. This would permit an interim subsidy of exchanges with higher costs per customer. S. 611 would establish a basic exchange maintenance program funded from access charges and provide an additional subsidy to small companies with less than thirty subscribers per route mile. About 1,000 of the independent companies would share an estimated $200 to $300 million under this provision. S. 622 would establish an access compensation charge to maintain reasonable rates for basic voice-grade telephone service through a fund administered by the participating common carriers, but the charge and fund would be terminated in six years or sooner if marketplace competition will maintain reasonable rates. The access charge in H.R. 6121 would not be phased out in any fixed time, and it would be used to fund basic telecommunications service at reasonable and affordable rates and to maintain reasonable access to interexchange facilities.

Kahn and others suggest that a larger proportion of families could be served if phone companies offered a lower-cost, basic-budget service for families that don't need to place 100 calls a month—so-called "life-line service." Some argue there is no justification for subsidizing all residential telephone service of all types. Moreover, they argue that eligibility for subsidies should be determined by the government and not by private enterprises.[44]

Henry P. Geller, assistant secretary of commerce for communications and information, argues that the social goal of universal service can be met through adjustments in pricing methods and, where necessary, through explicit subsidies.[45] He suggests that, in the long term, satellites and improved technologies may lower the cost of serving remote areas, but he admits other steps will be required in the meantime to ensure affordable service. S. 622 explicitly counts on competition and new technology to eliminate the need for subsidies after six years.

Proponents of deregulation and competition argue that the public interest standard of regulation for monopoly enterprises preferred by the established telephone companies is too imprecise, and even the industry has been surprised by the manner in which the courts have interpreted the term "public interest." The chairman of the House Communications Subcommittee has said that what now exists in communications is government by court edit.[46] Proponents of deregulation and competition argue that too often "public interest" regulation has been used to protect businesses from competition.

Some proponents contend that the system of cross subsidies through separations in the telephone industry is a "Robin Hood" method of redistributing income from business customers, who are heavy users of long distance services, to residential customers, many of whom could afford to pay higher bills. Inflated long distance rates, they assert, add to business costs and thus could contribute to higher prices for the goods and services that consumers buy. In their view, allowing free entry should permit service of underdeveloped submarkets, thus expanding the total market; this may also benefit established carriers. Consumers, they say, are in the best position to judge if services of established carriers are currently adequate.

**Affordable Rates and Equity.** Kahn cites Bell System figures that between 1940 and 1968 local telephone rates went up only 51 percent while the cost of living was going up 148 percent; in real terms, he says, local rates went down 40 percent. Olson contends that since 1967 the cost of living has doubled but rates for interstate long distance calls have gone up only 10 percent and that real interstate rates are 45 percent less than in 1967.[47]

Opponents of deregulation and competition emphasize that with a regulated monopoly public interest is paramount. The telephone companies may risk substantial losses but they can never make more than a reasonable profit as set by regulatory authorities. De Butts asserts that the objective of the telephone companies is the widest availability of high quality communications service at the lowest cost to the average user.[48] The current system of rate averaging, value-of-service pricing for business phones, and subsidy of local phone service through the separations process, it is argued, keeps home service at affordable rates. One witness claimed that many small independent companies could not continue in business if it were not for the revenues accruing to them from separations settlements. The president of Eastern Oregon Telephone Company is quoted to the effect that after all expenses are paid, money collected from the local exchange rate leaves his company with monthly losses on service of $5.02 on the business telephone, $5.92 on the telephone for an urban residence, and $14.58 for a rural residential telephone. According to its president, this company makes a profit on toll revenues due to the separations settlement procedure of $37.72 for the average business telephone and $1.88 for the urban residence telephone, while the rural residential telephone produces a loss of $6.55.[49]

Spokesmen for the Bell System argue that monopoly provision of telephone service under government regulation provides more affordable rates because the business is a natural monopoly which enjoys significant economies of scale—that is, it requires large fixed costs but unit costs decline as volume of service increases, and the benefits of these economies are passed on to telephone users. A large single system, they contend, can purchase or manufacture products and materials in large quantities at substantial savings. Telephone service is a high technology service that requires large amounts of capital; according to Bell, a large system can manage borrowing to obtain more favorable interest rates than would be possible otherwise.

Duplication of facilities through competition would be wasteful, it is asserted, and this would increase costs for all telephone users. Competition would reduce demand for Bell System facilities, so its unit costs would go up. Many facilities, such as standby facilities for use in emergencies, would be required even if fewer customers used the system. Bell cites a Stanford Research Institute study which argues that competition by specialized carriers through selective entry and selective pricing has not developed new markets but has simply captured business that had been handled by Bell.[50]

The most dramatic savings in telephone costs through economies of scale have occurred in long distance service.[51] In Bell's view, if the separations process were abolished, significant economies of scale realized by Bell Long Lines would no longer be shared by other independent and affiliated operating companies and their subscribers.[52] Local exchanges would be left with the high-cost part of the business. Bell had warned in the early stages of the debate over competition that local rates could increase as much as 70 percent if competition is sanctioned.[53] If increased costs cause a loss in residential users, it is argued that business telephones will be less valuable and business users may be unwilling to pay the exchange rates they now pay, thus forcing even higher rates for home telephones. Some business users, it is feared, might switch a substantial part of their business to other methods of communication.

Advocates of deregulation and competition contend that the natural monopoly argument is overworked. They argue that there are several reasons why long distance telephone rates have gone down in real terms. According to Kahn, one reason is the low-cost capital that some companies obtain through REA and the Rural Telephone Bank; another is the high rate of technological progress.[54]

In the view of proponents of deregulation, the reason there is only one dominant firm in an industry is due not to advantages of natural monopoly but to its protection by regulatory authorities which have refused entry to competitors. In their view it is wrong to entrust so much power to one concern. Some critics argue that regulators tend to become captives of the industry as the regulated firms develop liaisons with the staff and members of the congressional committees that deal with the regulatory agencies and as the firms become acquainted with the staff and commissioners of the agencies themselves.

Rate base regulation, it is said, rewards the companies that invest in excessive capacity. But proponents of competition ask if we are not paying too much for this fantastic capacity.[55] Henry P. Geller argues there is a danger the regulated industry will evolve into a "cost plus" operation. Rates will be set to recover all costs and a percentage of costs for a profit, thus encouraging the regulated companies to inflate the cost base on which rates are set; this approach discourages efficiency, innovation, and risk taking.[56]

Proponents of competition argue that the survival of specialized carriers in the market shows that AT&T lacks significant cost advantages. When businesses become too large, many exhibit managerial diseconomies of scale. Duplication of facilities, it is claimed, is not necessarily a sign of inefficiency in an industry, for if there is no duplication there may be excess capacity which could be a source of inefficiency. Competition, it is said, helps keep prices down even in regulated industries.[57]

Proponents of deregulation also contend that economies of scale and natural monopolies can be destroyed by changes in technology such as the development of microwave transmission which is less capital intensive than cable transmission. In any event, they say, if such economies do exist there is no need to erect legal or policy barriers to entry by new firms, since economies of scale will serve as a barrier to entry.[58] The Bell claim of rate increases of up to 70 percent is discounted by proponents of competition.

Kahn states that such a figure assumes that Bell would lose not only all new business but its existing interstate business as well, which is highly unlikely.

Those who support deregulation not only argue that competition may bring lower rates but also that ending the subsidy of local exchanges through the separations procedure would promote equity in rates. The separations formula may have saved state regulatory commissions the embarrassment of approving higher and higher local exchange rates to reflect actual costs of service, these proponents say, but MTS and WATS rates are higher than necessary and this is unfair to users of these services. Proponents of competition view the present rate and separations arrangements as a huge income transfer program. In their view we should not be subsidizing the wealthy along with the poor. They argue that it would be more equitable to permit competition to force rates down to the proper level, and to provide a direct subsidy for lifeline service to the poor so we can know exactly how much the subsidy is costing.

All of the pending bills would continue the policy goal of universal service at affordable rates. Their sponsors do disagree as to how the goal can best be met.

**Innovation and Quality of Service.** The way to promote innovation and high-quality service is a point of contention in the current debate. H.R. 3333 calls for universally available telecommunications services that are diverse, reliable, and efficient. S. 611 reiterates the current act's goals of universal, rapid, and efficient service; it also notes that technological developments promise a wide range of alternatives capable of satisfying diverse and specialized needs. S. 622 would ensure the minimum universal capability to provide basic voice-grade telephone service to all people and stresses promotion of maximum efficiency, flexibility, and versatility. H.R. 1580 finds that the technical integrity of the telecommunications system and its coordinated planning and management are indispensable and stresses the policy objective of an integrated network to provide high quality service to all users. H.R. 6121 would rely primarily on the private sector to determine the variety and quality of telecommunications services, facilities, and products in promoting the objectives of competition and universal and diverse services.

Proponents of deregulation and competition contend that a monopoly firm protected by regulatory authorities is not as innovative as are firms that must compete for customers. In their view, rapid innovation can help cut telecommunications costs over time, just as technological advances have cut telephone costs in the past in real terms.[59] Moreover, in their view innovation can improve the quality of service and add to the variety of products and services available to meet business and other needs. According to these proponents, specialized common carriers competing for business have gone to substantial lengths to tailor their services to the particular needs of business customers. Competitors of the Bell System have produced significant advances in such areas as PBX switching systems technology, fully automated processing of credit calls, and the digital switched network.[60] In their view, the technology to improve the quality and availability of service and reduce telecommunications costs in the long run is here now; competition in the marketplace can speed its availability to telecommunications users.

Proponents of deregulation contend that a single monopoly firm will not want to innovate rapidly because any new products may render its old products obsolete. Regulators seldom force a monopoly firm to offer innovative new services. Some economists suggest that regulation actually reduces the incentive to innovate because regulators often prefer to limit costs.[61] One witness, while admitting that Bell technology is top-flight, contended that competition has been the key element in allowing his nationwide merchandising firm to move ahead rapidly with innovative business systems.[62] In addition, proponents contend that competition stimulates the Bell System to respond to marketplace needs.[63] In sum, proponents regard competition as the means most likely to promote the objectives of greater innovation and greater diversity of products and services.

Spokesmen for the established telephone companies claim that their telephone network is a finely tuned, technologically sophisticated system of high quality. Critics and admirers of the system admit that it is the most reliable system of any nation in the world. Opponents of deregulation and competition insist that Bell has been in the forefront of innovation and the incorporation of new technology that is fully compatible with the existing system.[64] Their fear is that competition will hurt the integrity of the integrated telecommunications network and degrade quality of service.[65]

These arguments were made to the FCC when it was considering whether to allow competition in the provision of terminal equipment. The established telephone companies complained that inferior or incompatible equipment or faulty attachment of equipment might affect the performance of the system for millions of subscribers. The FCC chose to permit competition, but it issued standards and required the registration of equipment sold for user attachment to the system. Telephone company witnesses indicate that inferior equipment is in fact being attached to the system and when that equipment causes problems subscribers call on the telephone companies for assistance when in fact the trouble is not in the system.[66]

H.R. 1580, containing some of the provisions of the Bell bill (see, for example, H.R. 12323 and S. 3192 in the 94th Congress),[67] would give the states rather than the FCC jurisdiction over terminal devices and enumerated equipment. The only exception would be the limited circumstance in which the FCC finds after an evidentiary hearing that the use or connection of the devices or equipment has a direct and material impact on the technical integrity and capacity of the coordinated nationwide telephone network. H.R. 1580 would prohibit the FCC from authorizing any permit, license, or certificate for the operation of any telephone or telegraph common carrier unless it finds not only that authorization is required on the basis of present or future public convenience and necessity but also that the action proposed will not significantly impair the technical integrity and capacity of the coordinated nationwide telephone network.

As to innovation in telecommunications, the Bell System cites an Arthur D. Little study as showing that there is little empirical evidence that an increase in the number of telecommunications firms would spur innovation. Rather the Bell System has carried out a purposeful and systematic program of innovation for many decades that has produced numerous important technological developments.[68] The established telephone companies believe that unified responsibility for the entire system and the equipment attached to it will fix responsibility for quality and enable the Bell System to proceed in an orderly fashion with its research and development.

In the view of the established telephone companies, the goals of diversity and reliability stated in some of the reform bills are contradictory; they argue that diversity will be gained only at the cost of lowered standards of reliability. Smaller firms, it is said, will lack the resources for research and development needed to bring about major developments in technology. The established telephone companies contend that most of the innovations claimed by competitors are merely repackaging of existing technology. Bell spokesmen grant that this product differentiation can be of benefit to users but argue that research concentrating on marketing appeal may overlook innovation that is fundamental to reducing long-range costs of service and improving the quality of the network. According to Paul H. Henson, chairman of the board of United Telecommunications, Inc., fiber optics, though very promising, cannot be extended to local exchange operations within his lifetime at an affordable price unless national telecommunications policy bans competition in the provision of facilities.[69]

Proponents of competition and deregulation view H.R. 1580 as increasing the regulatory burden and discouraging competition. They fear that under that bill state regulatory agencies will in fact limit terminal attachments and authorized equipment to those developed and produced for Bell. They deny that the innovations produced by competing concerns are limited to repackaging for marketing appeal.

## Selective versus Universal Competition

The FCC initially opened two areas in the field of nonbroadcast telecommunications for competition. More recently it has moved toward deregulation and competition in a number of additional ways. Moreover, court decisions interpreting the 1934 act have made it more difficult for the FCC to limit competition, even if it chose to do so.

Congress has three options: it can go beyond the FCC's moves toward competition; it can reestablish monopoly provision of services and equipment for the future; or it can designate selected areas in which competition is justified. This section will examine the arguments for and against a selective approach to competition as opposed to competition in all aspects of non-broadcast telecommunications.

The first question in any debate concerning selective versus universal competition is how to justify the method of determining which areas of telecommunications will be subject to competition and which will not. One approach would permit competition only in areas where competition by itself would provide sufficient price discipline to protect the public, since this would permit elimination of a greater percentage of government regulation with the least economic risk to the public. Of course, few can effectively predict how competition would regulate an industry long dominated by a single family of companies. Areas could be selected for competition on the basis of the technologies involved, such as satellite and so forth. Some suggest that selection could be made on the basis of the areas most likely to produce and benefit from innovative services or product differentiation. Services that benefit most from economies of scale might be set aside for regulation rather than free competition.

In response to a question from Senator Schmitt as to whether a boundary could be drawn between areas where competition might be detrimental to the telecommunications industry's infrastructure and other areas that might be open to competition, then Chairman de Butts of AT&T responded that he would exclude from competition areas that exhibit significant economies of scale and scope, areas where competition would undermine an industry structure that meets congressionally established goals (presumably universal service at reasonable rates), and areas where the potential hazards to the national telecommunications system from competition so outweigh the potential benefits that the risk is not worth taking. Under this rationale, de Butts would exclude from competition the provision of local exchange service including a carrier-provided telephone, the provision of virtually all transmission facilities, the provision of ordinary long distance telephone service (MTS), and the provision of services which substitute for MTS in a manner to prevent use of separations from the MTS service to keep local telephone rates low.

This suggested boundary, in the view of de Butts, would permit competition in the manufacture and supply of telecommunications equipment and terminal equipment, except for one carrier-provided telephone instrument for each user. Competition would be allowed for unique services that could not be substituted for MTS or local exchange services. Similarly, transmission facilities that do not duplicate the network facilities or do not serve the same geographic locations could be subject to competition.[70]

In the view of Bell System spokesmen, such an approach would permit centralized control, coordinated planning, and joint operation of the nation-wide core public switched network through which jointly offered services would be provided under common tariffs. Nationwide service to meet the universal service mandate is said to require a nationwide system. Just as a systems approach of establishing clear goals and priorities and developing workable plans and procedures helped put a man on the moon, so, it is claimed, this approach would maintain quality telephone service for substantially all of the people at reasonable rates.[71]

If some such boundary is not drawn, telephone company spokesmen fear that unregulated competitors would select the high-volume routes over which service can be provided at lower cost and higher profit. Bell, hampered in competition by its regulation as a dominant carrier, would then be left with inadequate revenues to provide universal service at reasonable rates. Its own costs would increase as its economies of scale are eroded by lower volume, leaving it burdened with the debt incurred in building and maintaining a nationwide plant. Competitors would not be burdened with similar plant and debts.

According to Bell spokesmen, competition would lower the rates for only a few companies and a limited number of telecommunications users; the mass of telephone users would be disadvantaged. Bell representatives contend that universal competition would present other problems as well. They say that even selective competition has had an adverse effect on the value of Bell stock [72] and that universal competition would make it more difficult and more expensive to raise money for needed expansion and improvement of the network. Added costs of borrowing will have to be recovered from users in one manner or another.

Moreover, opponents of deregulation claim that competition will force Bell to stop thinking about the total market and to start concentrating on the more profitable aspects of the business to the disadvantage of universal service.[73] Some argue that where there are significant economies of scale for the Bell System, or the revenues from a particular clientele or area would not support two companies, it is not right to allow entry by companies who, after expensive duplication of facilities, will be forced out of business even if the competition is closely refereed.

Advocates of universal competition concede that some aspects of the provision of telecommunications services are essentially a monopoly and may remain so for some years. They contend that, under the pending bills to stimulate competition in telecommunications, the public switched network now provided jointly by the telephone companies would remain intact.[74] The registration program can ensure compatibility of equipment. They do not see universal service threatened. In the long term they propose subsidy of lifeline service for needy households.

They view the boundary proposed by de Butts as an arbitrary one designed to protect as much of the market for Bell as possible. They assert that advances in technology have removed old boundaries. In their view, technologies are merging and there is no easy or rational way to limit competition to certain areas or technologies. Competition is desirable, they contend, for the reasons outlined in the previous section and they see no reason to limit competition to particular segments of the market. If the Bell System truly enjoys economies of scale in certain areas which are overwhelming, Bell has nothing to fear from competition in those areas.

Proponents of deregulation argue that some competitors may not succeed, either because of Bell economies of scale or because a particular market will not support two companies, but they contend that this likelihood should not be used to limit competition. If a community can only support one drug store, would we deny a competitor the right to open another in the attempt to be the surviving store through lower prices and better service?

Some advocates of competition contend that much of the telecommunications market is devoid of economies of scale. Even if economies of scale do exist, they argue, consumers can also reap significant benefits from economies of specialization by competitors.[75] Competitors who do not have the same economies of scale enjoyed by the Bell System may still be able to earn a profit at prevailing rates if those rates are above the costs of the Bell System.[76] This would not disturb Bell's rate structure or interfere with any cross subsidy to local exchanges required by access charges. For the reasons outlined in the section "Fairness of Competition," advocates of universal competition do not see that the Bell System has suffered any significant handicap due to competition.

## Fairness in Competition

The interests of consumers of communications services is the principal focus of debate over telecommunications policy. However, the pending bills also try to protect competitors in the telecommunications market from unfair competition. This section will examine some of the major concerns with respect to fairness of competition and will explain how each bill deals with these concerns. While the full consequences of changes in the law cannot always be foreseen the effect of the various proposals on the fairness of competition does have a direct bearing on the practicality and equity of the proposals.

**Predatory Pricing.** In a classic case of predatory pricing, a firm prices its product or service below cost in order to drive other firms out of the market or to keep them from entering. The firm expects that the profits it can make in the future as a monopoly supplier will more than make up for its current losses. But if competitors can reenter the market and the period of freedom from competition is too short, the firm may have to engage in predatory pricing repeatedly, increase its interim losses, and risk detection and prosecution. Thus, many economists believe that the financial motive of monopoly profits is not enough to encourage predatory pricing and that such pricing is unlikely and even irrational.[77]

However, predatory pricing is said to be more likely when a firm's plant is used for both competitive and noncompetitive services. In that case, cost allocations for competitive and noncompetitive services are somewhat arbitrary, and higher profits in a monopoly market can compensate for losses in a competitive market. Continual predatory pricing to retain or attain monopoly position would be possible, subject, of course, to the risk of detection.

Four of the pending bills seek to open up the provision of telecommunications services to competition on a broad scale. However, their sponsors recognize that effective competition may not be attained in some areas for a substantial period of time if at all. Many of those who would compete with Bell are concerned that Bell may engage in predatory pricing practices to maintain its market dominance in the telecommunications field.[78] They claim that more than 90 percent of Bell System revenues are derived from monopoly services, and that Bell dominates competitive services even though these services produce a small part of Bell's total revenues. Because these competitive services provide some Bell competitors virtually all of their revenues, predatory pricing by Bell could destroy some competitors and extend Bell's monopoly power.[79]

How does Bell price its competitive services? In recent years, when the Bell telephone companies responded to competition by filing rate changes, they figured these rates on the basis of a long-run incremental cost (LRIC) methodology. This method projected the additional costs the equipment or services involved would impose on the company. Competitors claimed that this method failed to incorporate costs such as overhead and that Bell estimated future expenses subjectively rather than allocating its historical costs. According to competitors, this method would let Bell hide part of the costs for new services in the rate base for traditional services when some of the same facilities are used for both services. They note that Bell does not use this method to calculate rates for its monopoly services; if Bell were to do so, they observe, Bell companies would soon be bankrupt.[80]

In disallowing Bell's Telpak private line tariff, the FCC concluded that Bell's LRIC pricing was discriminatory because it was proposed only for competitive services.[81] The FCC ordered Bell to adopt a fully distributed cost standard for competitive interstate service offerings. Rates would then be based on the direct cost of a service offering plus a proportionate share of the company's expenses that could not be attributed directly to any service. Rates that have been submitted on this basis are said to be higher in each case than those based on the LRIC method.

Spokesmen for the Bell companies deny that Bell pricing in competitive markets is predatory. They argue that Bell tariffs filed before competition included more than the direct cost of equipment or services in order to support lower residential rates for users through the separations process, a cross subsidy fostered by regulatory authorities to further the universal service mandate.[82] In their view, the FCC has kept Bell's prices for competitive equipment and services unreasonably high as an umbrella to protect Bell's competitors. As a result, Bell claims one of the presumed benefits of competition—a more efficient use of the society's resources—is lost. Under perfect competitive conditions firms maximize profits (or minimize losses) by pricing which reflects marginal cost (the added cost of producing the last unit of equipment or service sold), and in ordinary competitive markets companies can price on this basis across the board and recover their total costs. In the telecommunications market, it is claimed, the tremendous investment required of Bell means that its total cost for a unit of service or equipment may exceed its marginal cost on a full distributed cost basis. A form of incremental pricing to charge new services only on the basis of the total investment required to add these services is necessary if competition is to be fair, say Bell representatives.

Bell also points out that competitors seeking entry into the telecommunications market have not had to make the same heavy investments that Bell has made, since they do not have to provide universal service, and have selected the more lucrative opportunities in the context of earlier Bell prices.

According to some antitrust authorities, firms that cut prices to the marginal cost level in response to entry by competitors are not acting improperly. Even if the price does not cover overhead expenses or the cost of past investment, the firm is clearly not a predator, according to these authorities.[83]

H.R. 3333 tries to deal with the fears of those who would compete with the Bell System by requiring only dominant carriers such as Bell to be regulated. Only a dominant carrier would have to file tariffs with the regulatory agency. The bill would also require AT&T and its affiliated companies to deal with each other on an arm's-length basis and offer products, services, or facilities to other companies on the same terms on which they are provided to members of the Bell System. Separations payments would be eliminated. Dominant carriers would have to permit interconnection with their facilities and the network on reasonable request and could not discriminate as to rates, terms, or conditions of such service. Dominant carriers could not establish or enforce unreasonable restrictions on the resale or sharing of interexchange services. Provisions of the bills that deal with Bell concerns will be discussed later.

S. 611 would aid firms wishing to compete with the Bell System by establishing a rebuttable presumption that there are no basic technological, operational, or economic barriers to effective competition in the provision interexchange telecommunications service. Also, S. 611 would establish a two-level regulatory arrangement. Carriers that are not subject to "effective" competition and those that provide essential services that cannot be left to competition would be subject to the full weight of current regulatory devices and also regulation of switching equipment; AT&T would fit this category. Most competitors would be regulated only in the sense that they must file reports with the FCC. The separations procedure would be replaced. Carriers like AT&T would have to provide interconnection to competitors on request for an agreed charge; the FCC could set the charge if agreement could not be reached.

S. 622 would prohibit cross subsidy of monopoly and nonmonopoly services. The FCC would prescribe an accounting system to separately state revenues and costs attributable to such services. Separations would be replaced with a system of access charges and interconnection between toll services and local exchanges would be assured. The FCC would classify carriers according to the amount of regulation needed by each, but regulation would be eliminated over the course of six years.

H.R. 6121 would employ a two-level regulatory approach and require separate subsidiaries and special accounting procedures to ensure fairness in pricing.

**Unequal Regulation of Competitors.** Spokesmen for the Bell companies argue that if there is to be competition, then the established telephone companies should be allowed to compete on equal terms. According to Bell, the two-level regulatory schemes that are spelled out in H.R. 3333, H.R. 6121, and S. 611 and implicit in S. 622 would regulate the Bell System's prices of services, expansion of operations, interconnection, and so forth, but would allow competitors to enter the market freely and set prices at any level they choose. S. 611 would still permit the FCC to delay needed rate increases or tariffs for new services for the Category 2 carrier when it is not subject to "effective" competition, but competitors would know no such restraints. Even if the Category 2 carrier is subject to effective competition it would still have to file tariffs while its competitors would not. H.R. 3333 would require every dominant carrier to file tariffs but competitors could change prices and terms of service at will. H.R. 6121 would permit the Bell System to compete as an unregulated carrier in offering nonbasic interexchange services but the FCC could reassert its regulatory authority if there is a lack of effective competition or the FCC believes this would serve the "public convenience and necessity." Bell spokesmen fear that under a two-tier regulatory arrangement, regulatory authorities would hold Bell rates artificially high as an umbrella to protect competitors. The tendency of regulators to artificially protect new competitors through regulation can lead to cartel management, according to Geller.[84] Fair competition, Bell spokesmen claim, would be confused with protecting competitors of the established carriers.

Bell spokesmen argue that if the telecommunications industry is to enjoy the claimed advantages of competition, the Bell System must have the market structure and environment which will permit it to function competitively. Bell, it is said, should be allowed to meet price competition.[85]

According to Geller, if regulation is continued, administrative procedures may become a serious burden for the regulated competitor. Administrative hearings on services that use advanced technology may last longer than the service being investigated; this type of delay, he says, benefits the unregulated competitors.[86] Bell spokesmen confirm this problem, noting that competitors in the supply of terminal equipment have found it in their interest to challenge nearly every Bell tariff that has been filed whether or not challenges were justified. The lengthy hearings increase the already difficult problem of coping with regulatory lag.

S. 622, for example, makes no change in the common carrier status of the Bell System and, as one witness put it, a telephone company cannot leave town and go to another country.[87] The established telephone companies are obligated to serve less profitable markets under most bills while their competitors in the provision of private lines service, for example, are able to select the markets they consider to be the most profitable and engage in cream skimming. In any event the established telephone companies, both independent and Bell, claim they serve many markets that are among the less profitable. If the separations process were eliminated, the phone companies say, they would in time require higher rates and perhaps reduce service for users in these markets. These steps may hurt the established telephone companies' ability to maintain essentially universal service while competing with cream-skimming competitors.

Geller cites the problem of a competing carrier establishing a very low-cost but unreliable network. The established telephone companies, in the view of some, would be subsidizing this carrier because the pending bills would compel them to provide backup service in case of trouble in the new low-cost network and to provide for overflow traffic under interconnection requirements.

Interconnection requirements in the pending bills may also be unfair, according to some, because they may allow competitors to dump large amounts of traffic on facilities of the established telephone companies that were not designed to handle such volume. Bell spokesmen argue that wherever it is necessary to assure the public of a nationwide telecommunications capability, the service should be under regulation.[88] But if there is to be competition, they argue that it should be full and fair and the pattern of regulation proposed for the transition period to full competition will, in their view, favor competitors and hobble the established carriers.

On the other side, those who would compete with the Bell System argue that, with one entrenched carrier supplying some 90 percent of the long-haul communications, full competition by the new fellows on the block without regulation during a long transition period is not practical.[89]

Senator Hollings refers to S. 611 as a series of halfway houses, each with progressively less regulation, together with an orderly process for moving from one to another as competition develops. He argues that if we were to remove all regulation the probable result would be a speedy end to the budding competition that has begun to emerge. He refers to S. 611 as a giant handicapping scheme and argues that an intelligent, flexible handicapping system with built-in mechanisms for tightening or loosening the restraints as competition flourishes or flounders is precisely what the industry most needs during the next one or two decades of transition to what he hopes will be full competition.[90] S. 622 and H.R. 6121 would regulate the dominant carrier, but S. 622 would phase out regulation in six years. H.R. 6121 would permit a dominant carrier to operate like a nondominant carrier in markets subject to adequate competition, and would require reassertion of regulation for the public convenience and necessity or if effective competition ceases.

Geller argues for a ten-year transition period, after which telecommunications regulation would expire unless extended by Congress. Without such a provision, he argues, regulation would tend to become self-perpetuating.[91]

Proponents of the four bills to promote competition contend that the continued regulation of certain carriers is needed because of their overwhelming market position and the nature of the essential services they provide. Even though the bills would require established carriers to provide interconnection for competing carriers, it is claimed the bills would also assure the established companies that they would be paid fairly for interconnection.

Geller contends that problems that may arise if unreliable competing networks dump traffic on the established carriers' facilities can be dealt with through interconnection charges that provide for peak-load pricing and the establishment of standby service fees. He argues that the problem of dumping heavy traffic volume from competing interexchange toll networks on the facilities of the established companies at unexpected points is a problem faced by all firms in a free marketplace. Although the bills do not provide for this, carriers could be required to submit facilities construction plans to the regulatory agency to help reduce forecasting uncertainty. Local exchanges might be protected from heavy unexpected traffic from competing carriers by proper selection of the points of interconnection and through proper tariff and contract arrangements.[92]

The provisions of the pending bills that bear on fair treatment of the established carriers include the following:

H.R. 3333 would regulate dominant carriers for ten years, but once the regulatory agency determines that a market is substantially competitive, the burden would be on those who challenge a rate to show that it is unjust and unreasonable, thus aiding the established carriers in competing. The Bell System companies could price services by assigning costs on a prospective-cost basis rather than a fully distributed cost basis; in time, they would be able to use a long-run marginal cost basis, so the regulatory agency could not hold up Bell prices as an umbrella to shield Bell's competitors. More rapid depreciation of assets would be possible in fairness to the established carriers who would have to compete with new carriers that do not follow traditional depreciation practices.

S. 611 states as one of its goals the promotion of fair competition. That bill requires the FCC to lower the level of regulation for carriers such as Bell companies as competition develops and the need for supervision declines. Both H.R. 3333 and S. 611 attempt to provide expedited administrative proceedings, particularly for carriers subject to effective competition, to treat the established carriers more fairly. A dominant carrier could also elect to file a long-term facilities construction plan to eliminate separate certifications for numerous items of construction, thus avoiding regulatory lag for new facilities approval.

S. 622 would provide an access charge for interconnection with the facilities of established carriers, but this would be phased out in six years. Accelerated depreciation charges would be permitted under FCC oversight. Proposals to offer nonmonopoly services and to construct or expand facilities would be automatically authorized unless the FCC determines within ninety days that a substantial and material question exists as to whether the investment is in the public interest.

H.R. 6121 would let dominant carriers offer nonbasic services without regulation under certain circumstances, and those seeking to reimpose regulation on dominant carriers as to nonbasic services would have the burden of proof.

H.R. 1580 goes futher toward meeting the concerns of the established carriers. It contains a specific finding that all who provide common carrier telecommunications services should be subject to the same regulatory process. A compensatory charge under the Communications Act of 1934 would be defined as one that equals or exceeds the added cost of additional facilities required to provide the service; the FCC could not hold a compensatory charge to a certain level to protect traffic or revenues from a service offered or provided by another carrier. Those who would compete with the established carriers would have to establish in a full evidentiary hearing that the service, operation, or construction proposed is required by present or future public convenience and necessity and will not impair the technical integrity and capacity of the coordinated nationwide telephone network.

**Affiliated Organizations.** H.R. 13015 in the 95th Congress would have prohibited any concern engaged in providing a noncompetitive telecommunications service from manufacturing equipment used in any domestic common carrier service three years after enactment. This prohibition was intended to require AT&T to divest itself of Western Electric and to help equalize competition.

Section 331 of H.R. 3333 does not require divestiture but would require that each affiliated organization of any concern that owns or controls a dominant carrier deal with every other affiliated organization on an arm's-length basis and in the same manner it deals with nonaffiliated companies and other business organizations. Western Electric could still design, develop, and manufacture equipment for the Bell System, but this would be done on a direct contract basis rather than through the existing license fee arrangement, which the bill's authors say results in an automatic levy on all Bell companies.[93] If Western Electric or another affiliate in fact provides one of the Bell companies with any products, services, or facilities it would also be required to provide other persons with nondiscriminatory access at comparable rates and on comparable terms.

S. 611 would authorize the FCC to require a carrier to separate its telecommunications activities from its other activities or services, or from the nontelecommunications activities or services of an affiliate. The FCC could also require a carrier to separate telecommunications services that are subject to effective competition from those that are not.

The bill would also prohibit carriers like Bell from selling, leasing, or marketing telecommunications equipment or electronics equipment, information software, or information services except through a fully separated entity, unless the FCC determined after a hearing that accounting or structural safeguards would be adequate to allow effective competition and protect users. A "fully separated entity" is defined as one that does not share directors, officers, employers, financial structure, or facilities with any other entity or carrier under common ownership and control and that deals with such as with any unaffiliated entity or carrier.

S. 622 would authorize the FCC to control the relation of subsidiaries which engage in business activities other than telecommunications to their parent companies, but the FCC could not require divestiture.

H.R. 1580 seeks to preserve the structure of the telephone network by including a congressional finding that the network and its coordinated planning are indispensable and a declaration that an integrated interstate network shall be structured to ensure widely available, high-quality service to all of the nation's users.

H.R. 6121 would require separate accounting systems for costs of facilities and products that are subject to regulation and those that are not. Those who would compete with the Bell System are particularly concerned with the system's vertical integration. Most of its operating companies purchase most of their terminal equipment and much of their exchange plant from the Western Electric Company, which is owned by AT&T. Western Electric and AT&T in turn jointly own Bell Telephone Labs (BTL). According to one witness:

> Western Electric is looked upon as *the* supplier of the Bell System and equipment from an outsider is viewed as an aberration. If an outside manufacturer's equipment has a problem, it is viewed as a reason for not buying it or switching back to Western. If a problem with Western's equipment is perceived, all of the resources of AT&T, BTL and Western are available to solve the problem. Western Electric is the only manufacturer that receives the full benefits of

> the systems engineering and fundamental research performed by BTL. These BTL functions and the entire AT&T General Department are funded by payment of a license fee by each Bell operating company out of its operating revenues. Only Western Electric can have new products developed by BTL. The Bell operating companies are encouraged to look only to BTL and Western for the technological innovations necessary to continue to provide high quality service at reasonable cost.[94]

Western Electric also serves as purchasing agent for equipment purchased from other manufacturers. Competitors in the sale of equipment have had to concentrate their efforts on sales to end users. According to some, Bell uses its vertical integration and in-family purchasing policy to constrain the growth of competitors and eliminate them.

Some Bell spokesmen have claimed that the decision to buy equipment almost exclusively from Western Electric was based on a price test that showed Western Electric products to be cheaper. Because Western Electric has what critics refer to as a captive market, it can anticipate sales volumes that would justify lower prices. In addition, it presumably obtains technological information from Bell Laboratories that competitors do not possess.

Some believe that Western Electric sells equipment for which there is competition at unreasonably low prices and makes up the difference with excessive charges on monopoly equipment. Those who wish to compete in the sale of equipment contend that Western Electric's overwhelming market share would permit it to destroy smaller rivals. Thus, divestiture is an appropriate remedy, according to some, and these critics argue for splitting Western Electric into smaller parts after divestiture.[95]

Some critics of Western Electric's relationship with Bell are primarily interested in being able to buy their own equipment from Western Electric. Cooperative and independent telephone companies complain that they have been forced to buy equipment at higher prices and lower quality from other suppliers.[96] A spokesman for competing equipment suppliers contended that Western Electric was selling to Bell companies at 40 percent under the price of competitive equipment.[97]

H.R. 3333, H.R. 6121, and S. 611 would attempt to equalize competition by forcing arm's-length dealings between separate organizations in the Bell System; S. 622 would lodge authority with the FCC to accomplish as much. Thus, these proposals go well beyond the concern with Western Electric and would force fundamental changes in the relationships among all members of the Bell family. Supporters of this approach feel that it is necessary to prevent cross subsidies and to ensure fair competition, since Bell currently lacks an adequate accounting system to fully segregate costs for various activities.

The chairman of the New York State Public Utility Commission argued that with fully separated subsidiaries there would be less need to engage in regulatory activities to prevent predatory pricing and so forth. When new markets are involved there is no loss of efficiency due to the requirement of a separate subsidiary, since there was no existing efficiency at risk. A representative of International Telephone and Telegraph Company argued that AT&T's Long Lines Division should be converted to a "carriers' carrier," similar to COMSAT's overseas operations. Other communications concerns would own an interest in the operation.

Henry P. Geller argued that the FCC should have the option of requiring use of fully separated subsidiaries but that such separate entities should not be mandated. Nor, in the view of some observers, would the separate statement of costs and accounts adequately protect against predatory conduct by a dominant carrier because, it is claimed, there is no unambiguous way to allocate or assign costs common to several services. The comptroller general has reviewed the FCC's four-year effort to implement a revised uniform system of accounts in the telecommunications industry and has concluded that the outlook for early implementation and effective use is dim.[98]

Bell System spokesmen respond to proposals for divestiture or arm's-length segregation of equipment manufacture and other Bell functions by denying any improper activity. The long-standing policy of the Bell System is said to be to "buy the best available equipment from any reliable source." Bell Chairman de Butts testified in 1977 that in the previous year Bell had bought $1 billion in equipment from outside suppliers.[99]

Bell claims that divestiture or other extreme measures would seriously harm Bell's efficiency, which Bell says derives from vertical integration of the Bell System and the close planning and coordination of its activities. Bell companies buy from Western Electric, it is claimed, because it offers the highest quality at the most reasonable cost and not because of orders from headquarters. Provision of services through totally segregated companies, Bell contends, would be wasteful since each company would have to have its own staff, its own financing program, and so forth. There would be a loss in economies of scale. Bell spokesmen claim it would be more efficient to establish accounting methods that minimize the potential for abuse rather than to rely on proposals which, even if adopted, would not satisfy Bell's competitors and critics.

Bell also argues that it should not be forced to give up vertical integration when some of its competitors and potential competitors will not have to do so. Vertical integration is said to be an important part of the systems approach to telecommunications service which has served the nation so well. The president of New Jersey Bell identified the benefits of the integrated structure of Bell as follows:

> It permits a "total systems approach" to the telephone service. Planning, research, invention, design, development, manufacture, and operations are directed toward a single objective.

It assures the necessary compatibility, reliability, and quality of equipment needed for optimum network function.

It facilitates and speeds innovation in the complex, interdependent network.

It assures that the demand for telephone equipment and service is met quickly and reliably.

It provides substantial cost advantages. In addition to the many other economies the Bell system achieves through integration, I would point out that Western Electric's prices for telecommunications products average about 20 percent below those of the lowest general trade supplier, thereby saving the Bell Operating Telephone Companies $1 billion per year.[100]

In the integrated structure, according to this witness, Western Electric orients itself to the goals of the system in furtherance of users' interests. Vertical integration also ensures the greatest degree of coordination among research, manufacturing, and marketing. This, says the president of New Jersey Bell, "allows for a free and open exchange of ideas and knowledge without the barriers of trade secrecy and conflicting interest. The Bell System and the independent telephone companies, because of their common commitment to service, have evolved a relationship facilitating optimization of the network under the technological leadership of the Bell System." [101]

All of these factors lead Bell officials to conclude that this relationship is responsible for Western Electric's lower prices and its high rate of productivity (about 3.8 percent increase yearly). The requirement of arm's-length dealings among Bell companies, they claim, would exclude Western Electric and Bell Laboratories from effectively participating in the planning and design of the system. Provisions such as Section 332 of H.R. 3333, which would permit any carrier to meet with any other carrier for planning and related purposes with notice to the attorney general and an opportunity for his representative to attend, according to a Bell spokesman, are not practical.[102] The cooperation and coordination that typifies network planning occurs at all organizational levels every day between literally thousands of people, they say. These activities could not be carried out on a timely basis in the manner proposed.

The chairman of AT&T contends that fully separated subsidiaries are unnecessary for another reason. Inefficient fragmentation or Balkanization of the telecommunications business could be avoided by detailed and closely supervised accounting systems that would prevent cross subsidy of competitive services from the earnings for monopoly services. Representatives of companies serving rural areas and Alaska also contended that requiring separate subsidiaries for various communications services would be unnecessary and costly and would seriously impair their ability to provide services.[103]

**Bell Entry into New Activities and Use of New Technologies.** The government's 1949 antitrust suit against AT&T and Western Electric was settled by a consent decree in 1956 which, among other things, restricted Bell to the provision of only regulated common carrier services. Western Electric could only manufacture equipment of the types bought by Bell operating companies for sale in the private sector. Whether some or all of these constraints should be lifted by legislation, as is proposed in H.R. 3333, H.R. 6121, and S. 611, involves the question of fairness to the Bell System and fairness to those who would compete against it.[104]

Currently, if a service is unregulated, Bell cannot compete by offering the service. Although the FCC may decide whether certain communications services should be regulated or unregulated, and thus may expand or restrict the services that Bell can offer somewhat, the FCC can only deal with communications services. Thus Bell is currently limited to providing regulated communications services.[105]

Bell spokesmen have also complained about FCC restrictions on its use of certain technologies within the regulated communications field. Other major corporations, such as Xerox and IBM, have entered the telecommunications market; some people believe that Bell should be allowed to compete against these and other concerns in the provision of information and computer services, for example. Geller and others agree that it is no longer wise to divide markets on the basis of technology.[106] Some observers see a vast new and rich market for data or computer communications and the merging of the broad computer and communications fields.[107] These observers claim that the lines between these two fields are blurred, as the FCC has found with its computer rules. As a result, a Bell spokesman observed:

> Attempts to make hard and fast distinctions between data processing and telecommunications will become even more difficult than they are at present. We can certainly identify what one might call "pure" data processing services that do not involve any telecommunications, and "pure" telecommunications services that do not involve any processing. But most of today's systems incorporate an important gray area between these "pure" extremes, involving elements of both telecommunications and processing.[108]

Bell spokesmen stress the need for greater flexibility to meet the communications needs of its traditional customers. If restraints on Bell are lifted, the result could be all-out competition in a wide variety of computer services.

Section 331 of H.R. 3333 would permit Bell (or any dominant carrier) and affiliates to engage in "unregulated telecommunications activities or other unregulated activities which are incidental to telecommunications," notwithstanding the 1956 antitrust consent decree.

S. 611 would provide that information or telecommunications equipment or telecommunications that AT&T or associated companies of the Bell System provide shall be considered to be regulated common carrier telecommunications services within the meaning of the 1956 consent decree. The bill would permit the Bell companies to provide information software and services in addition to its telecommunications services if the FCC found that conditions for effective competition in the relevant markets and the interests of telecommunications service consumers could be adequately protected by certain measures.

H.R. 6121 would permit the Bell System to provide unregulated services, facilities, and products, including data processing and the manufacture, sale, or lease of telephone equipment or terminal devices through separate subsidiaries with accounting systems to prevent cross subsidies, notwithstanding the 1956 antitrust consent decree.

Smaller computer concerns fear the consequences if Bell is allowed to compete outside the area of telecommunications. Philip Nyborg, representing the Computer and Communications Industry Association (CCIA), put it this way:

> Our members are angry and they are frustrated . . . because after two decades of existing at the sufferance of an industry dominant in the computer field which has not been effectively controlled by our antitrust laws, they now face the specter of market entry by a $38 billion government-sanctioned monopoly, AT&T. This entry is occurring now and moving forward daily with respect to terminal equipment, small computers, software and computer services.[109]

Nyborg believes that AT&T has marketed processing devices under the guise of "data transmission." But rather than permit the company to offer both kinds of services, he would require complete divestiture of a carrier's competitive and monopoly offerings.

> As long as monopoly carriers have the opportunity and incentive to subsidize competitive services within their own corporate family, anticompetitive subsidies will exist. And as long as any common carrier has the incentive and opportunity to favor other services or products within their own corporate family, discriminatory practices will be the rule.
>
> And I would emphasize that where multibillion-dollar corporations and multibillion-dollar market opportunities are involved, and indeed they are involved, the word "incentive" is a gross understatement. The economic pressures are *awesome,* and the ability of our regulatory system to deal with them . . . is minimal.[110]

H.R. 3333 tries to deal with the fear that Bell will compete unfairly through cross subsidy by requiring that a dominant carrier deal with affiliates at arm's length and that, if an affiliated company provides products, services or facilities to another affiliated company, it must provide other firms with nondiscriminatory access. Thus, if a Bell telephone company provides excess computer capacity to an affiliated company in the data processing business, it must make available equivalent capacity to other companies.[111]

H.R. 3333 would also bar a dominant carrier or affiliate from obtaining a radio license, unless the regulatory commission determines that a substantial portion of the relevant market would otherwise be unserved. Geller believes the regulatory commission should have the discretion to develop other structural requirements such as separate subsidiaries for Bell's noncommunications activities, and the authority to compel compliance, since the CRC will have no authority to regulate rates for services which are incidental to telecommunications.[112]

Geller argues that Bell, as a dominant firm, should be excluded from activities that have sensitive First Amendment implications. Its exclusion from mass media services (broadcasting, cable or pay TV, electronic publishing or newspaper services, or information retrieval) would also preserve or enhance diversity in the market.[113] Nondominant firms should, in his view, be free to engage in media activities as RCA and others do today. The broader authority for complete separation of the carriers telecommunications and nontelecommunications business is in fact provided in S. 611, and a fully separated subsidiary could not lease facilities from the communications affiliate except on terms that do not discriminate against the competitors of the subsidiary. H.R. 6121 requires separate affiliates and accounting systems to prevent cross subsidies when a dominant carrier offers unregulated services, facilities, or products.

As already noted, Bell spokesmen are concerned about the requirement for fully separated subsidiaries. They are also concerned that language as in H.R. 3333 permitting the regulatory commission to determine in disputed cases whether an activity is a telecommunications activity or is incidental to a telecommunications activity gives the agency too much discretion and too little guidance.

For his part, Geller objects to the provision of H.R. 3333 that would bar Bell from obtaining radio licenses for providing new radio telecommunications services (other than mass media services). The monopoly in local distribution of telecommunications may only be broken, in his view, by use of advanced radio services. While H.R. 3333 bars Bell in order to give others a head start in this field, Geller believes this would not promote open competition. In many instances, he notes, the dominant carrier may be in the best position to bring innovative radio services to the public. In other instances the dominant carriers may need to provide new services to meet competition from firms such as Xerox that are using radio to provide distribution of interexchange telecommunications.[114]

Cable TV systems are said to serve 12 million homes and an estimated 36 million people. Because of their broadband capabilities, cable systems can be used to carry digital signals and transmit computer data without devices required to convert such signals into signals that can be carried over voice-grade telephone lines. The majority of the lines of the established telephone companies are voice-grade lines employing analog signals rather than digital signals. In addition, cable systems can provide economical information storage and retrieval services and visual, facsimile, and telemetry transmission of all kinds.[115] Thus, cable systems may increasingly compete with the established telephone companies if the regulatory climate permits or encourages the provision of other than mass media services.

Cable systems have been heavily regulated in the past on the assumption this was desirable to protect broadcasters.[116] However, as can be seen from the above, cable systems can be significantly involved in nonbroadcast telecommunications functions. This raises the concern of fair competition between cable operators and established telephone companies for the provision of nonbroadcast services.

Three of the pending bills specifically deal with the role of cable systems in the nonbroadcast context. H.R. 3333 would permit cable companies to compete in the provision of all nonbroadcast telecommunications services, including basic voice service. Cable companies could also provide services incidental to telecommunications, such as burglar alarms, fire alarms, and data transmission. A dominant telecommunications carrier or affiliate could engage in cable activities, but only on an arm's-length basis; such a carrier would have to provide others with nondiscriminatory access at comparable rates and on comparable terms. A dominant carrier or affiliate would not be eligible for a license for a new radio system for the distribution of signals, but it could provide facilities for transmission of broadcast signals and for the provision of any electronic mass media service. The authors of H.R. 3333 feel this approach would permit telephone companies to enter the broadband service market and would eliminate the need for the current telephone cable cross-ownership rules.

S. 611 would permit cable companies to compete in the provision of nonbroadcast telecommunications services, but if they did so they would be regulated as are other telecommunications carriers providing similar classes of services. A cable company might be classed as a dominant carrier depending on whether there were other carriers within the same geographic market providing alternative or substitutable services. State authorities could set boundaries for cable intraexchange areas which are different from the intraexchange areas for telephone purposes, for example, and cable companies would not be subject to FCC jurisdiction unless they provided interexchange services. S. 611 would retain FCC authority for cable-telephone cross-ownership rules, so that telephone companies could be excluded entirely from the cable market or admitted on conditions.

S. 622 would include all cable systems within federal regulatory authority, though some activities would be unregulated and others would be subject to state regulation. FCC jurisdiction would be exclusive as to compatibility and interoperability of cable systems, equal opportunities by cable operators, and privacy of broadband communications, for example. Telephone companies would be prohibited from owning a cable system directly or indirectly. They could provide broadband transmission facilities to cable companies and others on a nondiscriminatory basis. The deregulation of cable systems proposed in S. 622 would permit them to compete in the provision of broadband services. The degree of state and local regulation which would be permitted over such services is not clear.

On the other side is the argument that telephone companies now find that the cost of installing coaxial cable is closer to that of the traditional twisted pair of telephone lines than it has been in the past. Thus the questions arise: If the telephone companies can install the higher capacity lines at nearly the same cost, should they be able to compete in providing a variety of broadband services? Would consumers, or just the investors, reap the benefits of the economies from such installations?

Arguments for or against telephone company ownership or operation of cable systems are linked primarily to the delivery of mass media services. However, the same arguments are applicable to nonbroadcast services as well. Assistant Attorney General John Shenefield of the Antitrust Division of the Department of Justice has expressed concern that allowing telephone companies to move into activities incidental to telecommunications might have profound effects on cable television. His fear was that the telephone companies might take over all cable television.[117]

The financial strength of the telephone companies is such that one witness argued minorities would not be able to compete with the established companies in urban markets.[118] Another witness argued for the exclusion of the telephone companies from cable TV as the best means of preserving a competitive environment for the development and use of broadband cable facilities and services.[119]

Witnesses from independent and cooperative telephone companies contend that the FCC prevents telephone companies from operating community antenna TV systems within their franchised territories. Cable companies do not provide service for many sparsely populated areas. Thus, it is claimed that only telephone companies can provide cable TV service in areas where there are as few as 3.4 telephone users per mile, to use one example, and residents in these areas should not be denied cable TV services in order to protect competition in another area.[120] Independent telephone companies may also be interested in diversifying into cable television, data processing, and other auxiliary activities, because if separations payments are phased out these companies will lose as much as half of their current revenues. Income from auxiliary services would cushion this loss.

# Notes to Text

[1] See Timothy E. Wirth, "Nation Facing Crucial Decisions Over Policies on Communications," *Congressional Record,* vol. 124 (July 12, 1977), p. E 4396.

[2] U.S. Congress, House of Representatives, Committee on Interstate and Foreign Commerce, Subcommittee on Communications, *Hearings on H.R. 3333,* 96th Congress, 1st session, May 1979 (hereafter *1979 House Hearings*), testimony of James E. Olson, vice chairman of the American Telephone and Telegraph Company, Attachment B, pages 2, 4, and 6.

[3] Specialized common carriers (SCCs) generally provide point-to-point private line telephone, data, and facsimile (exact copy of still pictures, charts, or printed material) communications. They provide part-time private line and single private line service to customers. They provide their own intercity transmission facilities but generally rely on the local telephone company for connection to the customer's premises. Carriers providing value-added networks (VANs) lease facilities from established carriers, add specialized services, and market this package to the final user. Domestic satellite carriers offer private line service comparable to that of the SCCs but, because they use satellites rather than microwave facilities for transmission, they have greater appeal for certain customers. Other firms provide public land mobile radio service. So-called miscellaneous common carriers deliver television signals to cable television firms and broadcast stations through microwave transmission.

[4] See U.S. General Accounting Office, *Developing a Domestic Common Carrier Telecommunications Policy: What Are the Issues?* 1979, pp. 4-6; "The Bell Family," *Congressional Quarterly,* vol. 34 (September 25, 1976), p. 2617; U.S. Congress, Senate, Committee on Commerce, Science, and Transportation, Subcommittee on Communications, *Oversight Hearings on Domestic Telecommunications Common Carrier Policies,* March 1977 (hereafter *1977 Senate Hearings*), pp. 160-163, Attachment B to testimony of Richard E. Wiley, chairman of the Federal Communications Commission.

[5] See 47 U.S.C. 151 and following.

[6] *1977 Senate Hearings,* p. 137, Attachment B to testimony of Richard E. Wiley.

[7] Ibid., pp. 1003, 1017, responses of Edward P. Larkin, commissioner, New York Public Service Commission and vice chairman of Committee on Communications of the National Association of Regulatory Utility Commissioners (NARUC) to written questions from the subcommittee chairman and attachment to responses; Ibid., p. 269, testimony of John D. de Butts, chairman of the board of American Telephone and Telegraph Company.

[8] *1979 House Hearings,* testimony of Paul H. Henson, chairman of the board of United Telecommunications, Inc., May 1, 1979, p. 16.

[9] Ibid., pp. 16-17.

[10] *1979 House Hearings,* testimony of Henry P. Geller, assistant secretary for communications and information, Department of Commerce, May 1, 1979, p. 21. 47 U.S.C. 410(c) adopted in 1971 calls for referral of proceedings involving jurisdictional separations to a federal-state joint board consisting of three FCC commissioners and four state regulatory commissioners nominated by NARUC.

[11] *1977 Senate Hearings,* pp. 248-249, opinion of Commissioner Benjamin L. Hooks in the FCC proceeding entitled "Economic Implications and Interrelationships arising from Policies and Practices Relating to Customer Interconnection, Jurisdictional Separations, and Rate Structures."

[12] Ibid., p. 606, testimony of Lee I. Davenport, president of GTE Laboratories, Inc.

[13] Ibid.

[14] *1977 Senate Hearings,* p. 1083, testimony of David Cossin, staff counsel for National Telephone Cooperative Association.

[15] Ibid., p. 277, testimony of John D. de Butts. Robert E. Sageman, executive vice president of AT&T's Long Lines Division, testified more recently that in the decade ending in 1978 separations payments had grown from $1 billion to $5 billion a year even though interstate telephone rates had only gone up 10 percent in the aggregate. U.S. Congress, Senate, Committee on Commerce, Science, and Transportation, Subcommittee on Communications, *Hearings on Amendments to the Communications Act of 1934,* 96th Congress, 1st session (hereafter *1979 Senate Hearings*), p. 424.

[16] Ibid., p. 492.

[17] Ibid., p. 41.

[18] Ibid., pp. 1212-1213, from a letter to Representative Timothy E. Wirth (D-Colo.) by the assistant attorney general for the antitrust division, dated January 19, 1977, submitted by Herbert N. Jasper, executive vice president of the Ad Hoc Committee for Competitive Telecommunications. See also Lawrence Mosher, "New Competitors with New Technology are Giving Ma Bell a Scare," *National Journal,* vol. 11 (April 28, 1979), pp. 691, 693.

[19] 47 U.S.C. 202.

[20] For a discussion of the pricing cases referred to in this section see *1977 Senate Hearings,* pp. 62-64, statement of Richard E. Wiley; *In the Matter of A. T. & T. Long Lines Department—Telpak,* 61 F.C.C. 2d 587 (1976); *In the Matter of A. T. & T.; Investigation into Lawfulness of Tariff No. 267, Offering a Dataphone Digital Service,* 62 F.C.C. 2d 774 (1977); Plaintiff's First Statement of Contentions and Proof and Defendants' First Statement of Contentions and Proof in the case of *United States* v. *A. T. & T., et al,* Civil Action No. 74-1698 in the United States District Court for the District of Columbia.

[21] *1977 Senate Hearings,* pp. 29-30.

[22] Ibid., p. 607, testimony of Lee I. Davenport.

[23] Ibid., p. 500, testimony of Alfred E. Kahn, chairman, New York State Public Service Commission.

[24] Ibid., pp. 640, 647, testimony of Walter Baer, senior physical scientist and deputy director of energy programs for the Rand Corporation.

[25] For background concerning the developments outlined in this subsection see *1977 Senate Hearings,* pp. 31-34, 100-104, testimony of Richard E. Wiley and Attachment B thereto.

[26] See Ibid., pp. 33-36, 62-64, 66-69, 115-119, 124-127. Radio Common Carriers (RCCs) have competed with the telephone companies in the provision of mobile radio services since the 1940s. At present there are about 500 RCCs competing with the telephone companies in this field.

[27] In employing packet-switching technology to service data communications needs of its customers, the VAN does not provide a customer with the exclusive use of a particular line or service. Rather, computers are used to arrange and store small groups (packets) of digitalized data for several customers and to forward such packets at high speeds over the best available path.

[28] *MCI Telecommunications Corp.* v. *FCC,* 561 F. 2d 365 (D.C. Cir. 1977), *cert. den.,* 434 U.S. 1040. The FCC's subsequent declaratory ruling that AT&T was not obligated to provide local physical connections for the Execunet service was overturned by the court of appeals which found support for its action in an earlier decision of another circuit. *MCI Telecommunications Corp.* v. *FCC,* 580 F. 2d 590 (D.C. Cir. 1978), *cert. den.,* 58 L. Ed. 2d 190; and see *Bell Telephone Co. of Pa.* v. *FCC,* 503 F. 2d 1250 (3d Cir. 1974), *cert. den.,* 422 U.S. 1026.

[29] William H. Jones, "Major Actions Taken by FCC to Deregulate," *Washington Post,* May 18, 1979.

[30] 47 C.F.R. 64.702.

[31] The 1956 consent decree settling the government's 1949 antitrust suit against AT&T limited the Bell System to the provision of regulated common carrier services only. Thus, the definitions in the rule cited in note 26 are critical to a determination of what is regulated and hence whether or not the Bell System can compete in offering various services. It was the view of FCC's Common Carrier Bureau that AT&T should not be permitted to market the Bell System's product Dataspeed 40/4. However, the full commission took a contrary view under its rule. It is expected that smaller businesses interested in competing for the growing computer services market and the Antitrust Division of the Department of Justice will challenge any final rule permitting computer services competition by AT&T, particularly in view of the latter's antitrust suit filed against AT&T in 1974. See Jones, "Major Actions Taken by FCC to Deregulate"; See also "Communications: Stretching Court Order to Permit AT&T Diversification Opposed," *Daily Report for Executives—Bureau of National Affairs* (hereafter *BNA–DER*), October 17, 1979, p. A-3.

[32] Larry Kramer, "In Telegrams Voted by FCC," *Washington Post,* January 26, 1979.

[33] The Justice Department's antitrust suit is captioned *United States* v. *American Telephone and Telegraph Company, Western Electric Company, Inc., and Bell Telephone Laboratories, Inc.,* Civil Action No. 74-1698 in the United States District Court for the District of Columbia. Senator Metzenbaum's concern is outlined in "Antitrust: Metzenbaum Warns of Competitive Problems with Communications Act Rewrite," *BNA–DER,* July 31, 1979, p. A-3. Senator Ernest F. Hollings's (D-S.C.) response to Senator Metzenbaum denying that S. 611 would constitute any kind of antitrust waiver appears in "Antitrust: Hollings Replies to Metzenbaum on Rewrite of Communications Act," *BNA–DER,* August 2, 1979, p. A-1. At issue is the question of committee jurisdiction in the Senate.

[34] Plaintiff's First Statement of Contentions and Proof filed in the case of *United States* v. *A. T. & T., et al,* Civil Action 74-1698 in the United States District Court for the District of Columbia.

[35] Defendants' First Statement of Contentions and Proof filed in the case of *United States* v. *A. T. & T., et al,* Civil Action No. 74-1698 in the United States District Court for the District of Columbia.

[36] *BNA–DER,* November 2, 1979, p. B-1.

[37] *1979 House Hearings,* testimony of Henry P. Geller, p. 2; *FCC* v. *RCA Communications,* 346 U.S. 86, 92 (1953).

[38] *1979 House Hearings,* testimony of Henry P. Geller, p. 2.

[39] One of the purposes listed by three of the bills is the promotion of competition. However, Senator Hollings argues that increased competition is a means to an end, the achievement of the other stated goals. "Communications Act Amendments of 1979," *Congressional Record,* vol. 125 (March 12, 1979), pp. S 2501, S 2502.

[40] *1979 Senate Hearings,* p. 1002, written responses of Edward P. Larkin to questions posed by the subcommittee chairman. For the special problems faced by certain rural operating companies and by the people of Alaska, see *1979 Senate Hearings,* pp. 479, 483, figures 1 and 3 from the statement entitled Rural Telephone Coalition Proposals for Telecommunications Policy Reform; ibid., pp. 531-532, 538-539, 542-544, 605, 667, statement of Ben W. Agee, president of RCA Alaska Communications.

[41] *1979 House Hearings,* testimony of James E. Olson, pp. 1, 6-8, 22 and Attachment A, p. 14.

[42] *1979 House Hearings,* testimony of Henry P. Geller, p. 26.

[43] Some advocates of deregulation and competition contend that apt as the universal service goal was in 1934 it is not sufficient for the decades ahead. *1977 Senate Hearings,* p. 497, testimony of Alfred E. Kahn; ibid., p. 1355, statement of Lee L. Selwyn, president of Economics and Technology, Inc. Selwyn contends that the universal service policy goal has largely been achieved and must now assume a secondary role. Senator Schmitt, after listening to committee hearings, has proposed an amendment to S. 622 to address the unique telecommunications needs of rural America. *Congressional Record,* vol. 125 (June 14, 1979), p. S 7738. See also S. 836 by Senator John Melcher (D-Mont.).

[44] See, for example, *1977 Senate Hearings,* p. 1289, written responses of Farrel D. Peltz, vice president for regulatory planning of the Codex Corporation, to questions from the subcommittee chairman. Peltz suggested that some new form of service such as a multiparty operator-assisted-only service or even a nonvoice instrument to summon police, fire, and medical assistance could be substituted for regular telephone services to assure basic service.

[45] *1979 House Hearings,* testimony of Henry P. Geller, p. 9; *1979 Senate Hearings,* pp. 245, 247, statement of Geller recommending the unbundling of services with local rates based on use instead of flat-rate pricing. Bell System officials, on the other hand, argue for the continued expansion of the concept of basic service just as a single-party line is considered essential today, though in 1934 an eight-party line was satisfactory. Ibid., p. 208, statement of Charles L. Brown, chairman of AT&T; ibid., p. 399, statement of Robert E. Sageman.

[46] Timothy E. Wirth, "Nation Facing Crucial Decisions Over Policies on Communications," *Congressional Record,* vol. 123 (July 12, 1977), pp. E 4396, E 4397.

[47] *1979 House Hearings,* testimony of James E. Olson, Attachment A, p. 18.

[48] *1977 Senate Hearings,* p. 268, testimony of John D. de Butts.

[49] Cited in attachment to testimony of Edward P. Larkin, *1977 Senate Hearings,* p. 1013.

[50] *1977 Senate Hearings,* pp. 304-305.

[51] Ibid., p. 606, testimony of Lee I. Davenport, president of GTE Laboratories. Davenport states that there are not as many opportunities for cost reduction in local telephone services through sharing of equipment and economies of scale and there are greater problems in speeding up service and delivering new types of service at the local level.

[52] *1979 House Hearings,* testimony of Paul H. Henson, p. 22.

[53] "Bell Telephone Presses Case for Monopoly," *Congressional Quarterly,* vol. 34 (September 25, 1976), p. 2615.

[54] See, for example, *1977 Senate Hearings,* p. 492, testimony of Alfred E. Kahn.

[55] Larry Kramer, "FCC's Ferris Looks Ahead," *Washington Post,* March 4, 1979.

[56] *1979 House Hearings,* testimony of Henry P. Geller, p. 3.

[57] *1977 Senate Hearings,* p. 647, written responses of Walter Baer to questions from the subcommittee chairman.

[58] Ibid., pp. 1159-1171, study of William H. Melody, professor and chairman of the Department of Communications Studies, Simon Fraser University, Vancouver, B.C., attached to testimony of Kenneth A. Cox, senior vice president, MCI Communications Corp.

[59] See, for example, U.S. General Accounting Office, *Developing a Domestic Common Carrier Communications Policy: What Are the Issues?* January 1979, p. 24; also the testimony of Alfred E. Kahn cited in note 64.

[60] *1977 Senate Hearings,* pp. 1055-1056, written responses of V.P. Moore, Jr., senior vice president, Securities Industry Automation Corporation, to questions of the subcommittee chairman; ibid., p. 1062, written responses of Robert Capone, vice president and director of systems and data processing for J.C. Penney Company; ibid., pp. 1094, 1101, 1104, 1107, 1126, statement of C. Gus Grant.

[61] For an application to telecommunications, see William Shepherd, "The Competitive Margin in Communications," in William Capron, ed., *Technological Change in Regulated Industries* (Washington, D.C.: The Brookings Institution, 1971), pp. 86-122.

[62] *1977 Senate Hearings,* pp. 1057-1058, testimony of Robert Capone.

[63] Ibid., pp. 1103, 1126, statement of C. Gus Grant. Also see Richard E. Wiley, quoted in "Bell Telephone Presses Case for Monopoly," p. 2616.

[64] See, for example, Larry Kramer, "AT&T Stays on the Cutting Edge," *Washington Post,* May 27, 1979; *1977 Senate Hearings,* p. 1291, testimony of Wilson Garnett, executive vice president, Central Telephone and Utilities Corporation, on behalf of the U.S. Independent Telephone Association.

[65] "Bell Telephone Presses Case for Monopoly," p. 2616.

[66] *1977 Senate Hearings,* p. 1086, testimony of Frank James, president, National Telephone Cooperative Association.

[67] The Bell bill is discussed in "Bell Telephone Presses Case for Monopoly," p. 2618. For Richard E. Wiley's critique of the Bell bill on behalf of the FCC see *1977 Senate Hearings,* pp. 82-90.

[68] *1977 Senate Hearings,* pp. 309-437.

[69] Ibid., p. 1323. Walter Baer states that technological developments are proceeding very rapidly but that it has taken fifteen years or more for many of these technologies to penetrate the system because enormous sums have been invested in plant and facilities. Thus, he predicts application of technology will be evolutionary and not revolutionary. Compare statement of Chairman Ferris of the FCC in Kramer, "FCC's Ferris: Looking Ahead" (note 55).

[70] *1977 Senate Hearings,* pp. 470-471.

[71] *1977 House Hearings,* May 1, 1979, testimony of James E. Olson, pp. 12, 22, and Appendix B, p. 5.

[72] See Dan Dorfman, "AT&T No Longer Investors' Sure Bet," *Washington Post,* May 9, 1979.

[73] *1977 Senate Hearings,* p. 267, testimony of John D. de Butts, p. 936; testimony of Edward P. Larkin.

[74] *1979 House Hearings,* May 1, 1979, testimony of Henry P. Geller, p. 28.

[75] *1977 Senate Hearings,* p. 1245, letter from Herbert N. Jasper, dated June 16, 1977, to the chairman of the Senate Subcommittee on Communications.

[76] Ibid., p. 1170, study of William H. Melody submitted as an attachment to the testimony of Kenneth A. Cox.

[77] John McGee reached this conclusion in his study of the most famous case of alleged predatory pricing—the Standard Oil trust. Standard's conviction was upheld in a precedent-setting opinion by Supreme Court Chief Justice Edward White in 1911, but, McGee argues, it is unlikely that Standard ever engaged in predation. See his "Predatory Price Cutting: The Standard Oil (N.J.) Case," *Journal of Law and Economics,* vol. 1 (October 1958), pp. 137-169.

[78] Claims of predatory pricing are heard most frequently in the terminal equipment market. In its suit to compel separation of Western Electric from the Bell System, the Department of Justice contends that the defendants have engaged in cross subsidization of competitive and monopoly services and equipment and in predatory pricing. Approximately thirty private antitrust law suits make the same claim.

[79] *1977 Senate Hearings,* p. 1166, study of William H. Melody, attached to testimony of Kenneth A. Cox.

[80] Ibid., p. 1171. Edwin B. Spievack, counsel to the North American Telephone Association, contended that "Bell's incremental pricing is merely a method to justify predatory pricing." Ibid., p. 1255.

[81] Federal Communications Commission, "In the Matter of American Telephone and Telegraph Company Long Lines Department," 38 Radio Regulations 2nd 1166 (1976). The FCC noted that even small errors in underlying projections could result in significant underpricing of competitive services or false entry signals for competitors. Ibid., p. 1156.

[82] Alfred E. Kahn testified that the New York Public Service Commission believes Bell terminal equipment offerings fall short of recovering costs. Though the issue is said to be complicated and hotly contested, in Kahn's view interstate rates bear the burden of the failure of terminal equipment to cover costs. *1977 Senate Hearings,* pp. 492-493.

[83] Philip Areeda and Donald Turner, "Predatory Pricing and Related Practices Under Section II of the Sherman Act," *Harvard Law Review,* vol. 88 (February 1975), p. 703; see also Richard Posner, *Antitrust Law: An Economic Perspective* (Chicago: University of Chicago Press, 1976), pp. 187-192. It is argued that, more importantly, such pricing can benefit consumers as well as the price cutter and, if new competitors cannot meet the lower price, they must be less efficient (have higher marginal costs) than the dominant firm. FCC's complaint that LRIC pricing was discriminatory because it was employed for competitive equipment or services but not for monopoly services is said by Bell spokesmen to ignore the findings of Baumol that rate reductions for competitive services do not necessarily burden the users of monopoly services. In Baumol's view a price for competitive services which is too high—for example, a price based on a fully distributed cost methodology—might lead to an erosion of the firm's market share and a reduction in the revenues available to offset fixed costs, costs which users of monopoly services would continue to pay in the absence of the other service. This "burden test" was discussed in William Baumol, et al, "Competition and Monopoly in Telecommunication Services," prepared for the American Telephone and Telegraph Company, 1970.

[84] *1979 House Hearings,* statement of Henry P. Geller, p. 16.

[85] Ibid., statement of Paul H. Henson, p. 18; *1977 Senate Hearings,* p. 298, analysis of issues and findings in FCC Docket 20003, prepared by Stanford Research Institute, attached to written statement of John D. de Butts.

[86] *1979 House Hearings,* statement of Henry P. Geller, p. 16. The Justice Department has accused Bell of using the current regulatory process to delay competitors seeking to become established in a market until it has developed its own competing offering. Carole Shifrin, "U.S. Now Contemplates Further AT&T Breakup," *Washington Post,* November 3, 1978.

[87] *1979 House Hearings,* p. 939, testimony of Edward P. Larkin.

[88] "New Competitors with New Technology are Giving Ma Bell a Scare" (see note 18), p. 693, quoting Charles L. Brown.

[89] Ibid., p. 694, quoting Stuart L. Mathison, vice president for business planning for Telenet. See also *1977 House Hearings,* p. 320, testimony of John H. Shenefield, assistant attorney general for the Antitrust Division of the Department of Justice, and p. 326, testimony of the former FCC Commissioner, Dean Burch.

[90] *Congressional Record,* vol. 125 (March 12, 1979), pp. S 2503, S 2504.

[91] *1979 House Hearings,* testimony of Henry P. Geller, p. 5, and p. 1 of the attachment.

[92] Ibid., pp. 30-31.

[93] House Committee Print 96-IFC 11, 96th Congress, 1st session.

[94] U.S. Congress, House of Representatives, Subcommittee on Communications of the Interstate and Foreign Commerce Committee, *Hearings on Revision of the Telecommunication Laws,* 95th Congress, 1st session (hereafter *1978 House Hearings*), testimony of Frank Barnes, vice president of ITT, August 3, 1978, p. 4.

[95] The FCC concluded an investigation of the relationship between Western Electric and the remainder of the Bell System in March 1977. Federal Communications Commission, "In the Matter of AT&T and the Associated Bell System Companies: Charges for Interstate Telephone Service," Docket 19129 (March 1, 1977). The FCC trial staff had recommended a divestiture but the FCC did not accept that recommendation or establish a quota for outside purchases. It did order AT&T to devise a plan that would give the operating companies more autonomy in buying outside equipment and ruled that Western Electric should give up its role of deciding specifications for the equipment supplied to the Bell System. The Justice Department's suit seeks to force AT&T to divest itself of Western Electric, its Long Lines Division, and some or all of the operating telephone companies; to split Western Electric; and to examine the relationship of Bell Labs.

[96] *1977 Senate Hearings,* p. 1080, testimony of Frank James.

[97] Ibid., p. 1256, testimony of Edwin B. Spievack.

[98] Ibid., p. 811, written responses of Herbert E. Marks, counsel for the Remote Processing Services Section of Association of Data Processing Service Organizations, Inc., to questions from the subcommittee chairman; *1979 Senate Hearings,*

pp. 261, 264, statement of Charles A. Zielinski, chairman, New York State Public Service Commission; ibid., 265, 361, statement of Henry P. Geller; ibid., p. 727, statement of George P. Knapp, vice president of ITT; ibid., p. 411, statement of C. Gus Grant, president of Southern Pacific Communications Company; ibid., p. 754, statement of James Lovell, North American Telephone Association; U.S. General Accounting Office, *Outlook Dim for Revised Accounting System Needed for Changing Telephone Industry,* November 1979.

[99] *1978 House Hearings,* testimony of Morris Tannenbaum, president of the New Jersey Bell Telephone Company, August 8, 1978, p. 14; Stephen M. Aug, "AT&T Lawsuit Defense: U.S. Misunderstands," *Washington Star,* January 9, 1978; *1977 Senate Hearings,* p. 281, testimony of John D. de Butts. More recent data are claimed to show that Bell System purchases from outside suppliers amounted to $8 billion in 1978 and that $1½ billion of these purchases involved telecommunications products and 75 percent of these latter purchases involved products similar to those manufactured by Western Electric. *1979 Senate Hearings,* pp. 200-201, statement of Charles L. Brown.

[100] *1978 House Hearings,* testimony of Morris Tannebaum, pp. 9-10.

[101] Ibid., p. 33.

[102] *1979 House Hearings,* statement of James E. Olson, pp. 9-10.

[103] *1979 House Hearings,* statement of James E. Olson, May 1, 1979, pp. 9-10, 18, 23. *1979 Senate Hearings,* pp. 194, 217, statement of Charles L. Brown; ibid., pp. 540, 786, statements of Ben W. Agee; and Glenn W. Bergland for the Organization for the Protection and Advancement of Small Telephone Companies.

[104] Whether the attorney general and the U.S. district court would assent to modification of the consent decree in the event of such legislation is an open question. See Stephen M. Aug, "Commerce, FCC Staff Push to Modify Curb on AT&T," *Washington Star,* February 22, 1979.

[105] *Congressional Record,* vol. 125 (March 12, 1979), p. S 2503.

[106] *1977 Senate Hearings,* p. 275, testimony of John D. de Butts; *1979 House Hearings,* testimony of Henry P. Geller, p. 9, and attachment, p. 7; testimony of Paul H. Henson, p. 24. Charles L. Brown argues that application of the antitrust laws should be suspended during the transition to full competition to the extent that they frustrate regulation or the introduction of competition in previously regulated markets. Geller contends that at a minimum Congress should provide that data or information processing and the sale or lease of computer terminals are incidental to telecommunications and that these may be provided by dominant carriers. He proposes that Congress explicitly overrule the 1956 antitrust consent decree to this extent and that the FCC be authorized to decide if other services are incidental to telecommunications. *1979 Senate Hearings,* p. 244.

[107] "Bell Telephone Presses Case for Monopoly" (see note 53), p. 2618. W. F. Redderson of AT&T is quoted as estimating that data communications revenues will grow from $5 billion in 1975 to some $22 billion in 1985, the latter figure being about the size of total Bell revenues in 1973. In the same period

revenues from data terminals are estimated to have increased from $2 billion to $14 billion. *1977 Senate Hearings,* p. 1143, from a paper of Manley R. Irwin, professor of economics at the University of New Hampshire attached to the testimony of C. Gus Grant. Some observers contend that companies that start out to sell data transmission end up selling more voice transmission than data transmission. Ibid., p. 597, testimony of John R. Pierce, professor of electrical engineering, California Institute of Technology.

[108] *1978 House Hearings,* testimony of Edward Goldstein, director of project management for AT&T, August 8, 1978, p. 10.

[109] *1978 House Hearings,* testimony of Philip Nyborg, August 3, 1978, p. 2.

[110] Ibid., p. 22.

[111] House Committee Print 96-IFC 11, p. 25.

[112] *1979 House Hearings,* attachment to testimony of Henry P. Geller, p. 8.

[113] Ibid., testimony of Henry P. Geller, p. 19.

[114] Ibid., attachment to testimony of Henry P. Geller, pp. 8-9.

[115] *1977 Senate Hearings,* p. 1076, statement of Ralph Baruch, chief executive officer, Viacom International.

[116] Ibid., p. 1063.

[117] *1978 House Hearings,* p. 310.

[118] Ibid., p. 540, statement of Ed Hayes, a lawyer formerly with Citizens Communications Center, a public interest law firm.

[119] *1977 Senate Hearings,* p. 1076, statement of Ralph Baruch.

[120] *1977 Senate Hearings,* p. 1083, testimony of Frank James; p. 1293, testimony of Wilson Garnett.